Foreword

THE READY REFERENCE POCKET MANUAL

Here's What It Is

A whole library of life insurance sales material condensed into a pocket-size book . . . tested sales ideas . . . power phrases that sell . . . facts, figures, charts, tables for sales presentations . . . new sales slants . . . sure-fire sales talks . . . tips from successful life insurance agents—truly a bookshelf of effective sales aids.

Here's What It's For

For use in preparing for interviews . . . in setting up proposals . . . in actual discussions with prospects . . . ideal for quick reference in your office . . . in the prospect's home or office . . . in moments of waiting for interviews . . . in any spare minute of the day.

Here's How You Use It

Suppose your next interview is with a prospect for **mortgage cancellation insurance.** Look up "Mortgage insurance" . . . flip to the pages that set forth the need . . . find a motivating visual . . . turn to the mortgage tables for helpful facts and figures . . . bolster your presentation with mortgage power phrases . . . study the practical answers to objections.

Use the same procedure for **business insurance . . . retirement plans . . . estate planning.** You'll never go away from an interview thinking, "If only I had remembered **that point . . . that figure . . . that answer to an objection.**" You can show the prospect the convincing phrase or fact or page that will clinch the sale!

But first, become familiar with the contents and arrangement of your Manual. **Study the Preface carefully.** See how the ideas and topics of information are organized logically so you can find them in a

Ready Reference Pocket Manual

Dearborn
R&R Newkirk
a division of Dearborn Financial Publishing, Inc.

Published by Dearborn • R&R Newkirk, a division of Dearborn Financial Publishing, Inc.

Printed in the United States of America.

First printing, February 1993

For information contact:
Dearborn • R&R Newkirk
520 North Dearborn Street
Chicago, IL 60610-4354

Library of Congress Cataloging-in-Publication Data

The Ready reference pocket manual/[Published by Dearborn • R&R Newkirk, a division of Dearborn Financial Publishing Inc.].
p. cm.
Includes index.
ISBN 0-79310-519-6
1. Insurance, Life—Agents—United States—Handbooks, manuals, etc. 2. Selling—Handbooks, manuals, etc. I. Dearborn • R&R Newkirk.

HG8881.R43 1993 92-43896
368.3'2'00688—dc20 CIP

hurry. **Then refer to the introductory text that precedes each chapter of the Manual.** It outlines the scope and purpose of the chapter and explains how the material can be used most profitably. **Next, turn to the Index at the back of the Manual.** Here is a general listing of subject matter that will lead you quickly to the desired pages.

Carry the Manual with you always. Make it a constant companion in your sales work. Take advantage of every opportunity to browse through the pages. You will be amazed to see how quickly you absorb and attain a mastery of many new sales techniques, almost without conscious effort.

The Dearborn•R&R Newkirk *Ready Reference Pocket Manual* is dedicated to you and to all life agents who endeavor to serve their clients more effectively.

Contents

Preface

SCOPE OF THE MANUAL

Know Your Prospect's Mind (Pages 2–22)

Uncover Your Prospect's Needs (Pages 23–80)

Locate and Contact Your Prospect (Pages 81–92)

Pointers toward the creation of a supply of prospects from your personal contacts. Also field-tested prospecting techniques for use with friends, policyowners, business persons, clergy members and farmers. Included in this section are many effective suggestions for the proper use of the telephone in securing appointments.

Motivate Your Prospects to Action (Pages 93–107)

Over 100 power phrases that top agents are using in opening interviews, motivating the prospect and clinching sales.

Anticipate Your Prospect's Objections (Pages 108–31)

Here are a variety of field-tested replies to objections commonly encountered in the interview. They will open doors and close sales. Have them at your fingertips!

Life Insurance and Other Investments (Pages 132–37)

Be prepared to explain the place of life insurance and its value as a base for a total financial plan on a par with equity investments. The purpose of this section is to help you show prospect that you are equipped to discuss both risk and guaranteed investments.

Total Needs Selling (Pages 138–61)

Suggestions for making your total needs selling interviews more effective. These hints apply to the four stages of the sales procedure—Approach, Fact-Finding, Solution and Close. Here are valuable ideas you can adapt to any method of programming you are now using.

Estate Protection (Pages 162–92)

Includes an outline of the steps in estate planning—an analysis of the problem of estate shrinkage, showing how life insurance solves the problem—a brief study of the instruments available for proper estate distribution.

Business Insurance (Pages 193–239)

A quick reference to help the agent in preparing for business insurance interviews. Covers Key-Person, Sole Proprietor, Partnership and Close Corporation situations. Also includes introductory material for group life, health and tax-deferred investment and pension/retirement plans. Can be used in the interview, itself, to illustrate certain business problems for which life insurance is the only adequate solution.

Retirement (Pages 240–48)

Opportunities for the sale of retirement funds to those who qualify—Keogh (HR-10) plans for the self-employed—Individual Retirement Accounts (IRAs), SEPs and 401(k)s are explained.

Some Sales Ideas (Pages 249–70)

Presenting three sure-fire sales ideas that are selling millions of dollars of life insurance: Deferred Compensation, Split-Dollar Arrangements and the $5,000 Death Benefit Only (DBO). Each is explained in simple language.

Charts, Tables and Sales Aids (Pages 271–302)

A compilation of charts, facts, tables, illustrations—covering many points that arise in the interview: settlement options, mortality tables and compound interest tables.

1

Being in Tune with the Prospect's Thinking

The successful agent is one who can "tune in" with the thought processes of the prospect. The successful agent wants to know how the prospect thinks. To understand the mind of the buyer is worth much in the interview. Use this section to analyze your prospects' thinking before you contact them.

Suppose you plan to call on a doctor. If you will study the sketch which deals with the characteristics of doctors and how they think, you can prepare a doubly effective presentation! The same suggestion applies to the other vocations and professions discussed here.

Accountants: They are factual, statistical and analytical. They admire precision and clear logic; they can follow a detailed presentation. The more businesslike it is the more they will believe in it. Definite plans, definite savings objectives appeal to them. Accent programming, monthly income; use charts and graphs. **But don't present figures you can't substantiate!**

Administrative Assistant (Also applies to secretaries, word processors, etc.): Surveys show that single people in these positions are most interested in permanent life insurance that can accumulate cash for definite objectives, such as a long trip, money for a home, money to pursue hobbies, or advance their careers, a nest egg for marriage, and of course, financial security in retirement.

Advertising Executives: Income depends on continued ability to produce effective sales ideas. In and out of the office, they are thinking, dreaming, planning. They need automatic investment plans that take care of themselves, and will be receptive to creative ideas.

Make your proposals attractive, interesting, colorful and neat. Talk about the **guarantees** of life insurance and the necessity for total financial planning. Emphasize the fact that the success of the agency depends on **brainpower,** the personal skills and abilities of the key personnel. This may lead to further discussion on business continuation and key-person insurance. (See Business Insurance chapter.)

Make your proposals neat, precise, and with as few confusing insurance terms as possible.

Architects: See **Professionals** in Chapter 2.

Artists (Commercial, Cartoonists, Illustrators, Musicians, Portrait, Sculptors): Emphasize retirement, because their earning years may be short: point out that their life value lies in their **skill,** and this value may steadily depreciate or be destroyed in a moment. Only life and disability insurance guarantee replacement of this value.

Attorneys: See **Lawyers.**

Auditors: See **Accountants.**

Bankers (Bank Executives): They know the value of financial security, of freedom from speculation, of guaranteed return on an investment, of the dangers that arise from either unexpected demands for cash or from unexpected death. They will respond to cold facts and figures, plus a reminder of disasters that they have witnessed among their clients—those who lost homes, or were forced to liquidate securities in an unfavorable market.

Use the same sort of factual, statistical presentation as you would use with accountants. Make sure your figures are accurate.

Brokers (Investment Counselors, Investment Salespeople, etc): These people caution would-be investors to have adequate life insurance, with its guaranteed values, before venturing into forms of risk investments. If sincere, their advice to their clients should also apply to themselves. Emphasize an **adequate** foundation of life insurance from the standpoint of income. Accent the advantages of life insurance that are not to be found in the field of investments. See Investments chapter.

Chiropractors: See **Doctors**.

Clerical Workers: Generally, clerical workers have a day-to-day routine, want to feel secure in their jobs, and are hesitant to venture into new fields.

Steady workers for steady, moderate pay, they need a regular cash accumulation plan to force them to take a constant amount from their paychecks to provide family protection and retirement income. Show them how relatively few dollars, paid regularly into an efficient plan, will accomplish much. Accent safety, security, guaranteed cash values, and guaranteed incomes plus the necessity for investing for the future. These values will appeal to the clerical worker.

Contractors: Contractors deal with big projects involving large sums of money. They may have thousands upon thousands of dollars at risk in contracts at one time. So talk **big** amounts — illustrate **big** results; don't make penny-ante proposals to contractors who are used to arranging big-money transactions.

And because large amounts of money are involved in the contractor's various projects, death of the contractor can mean tremendous losses, especially when a number of subcontractors have claims against the deceased for materials and labor. This calls for appreciable life insurance.

Contractors frequently have key people whose know-how and ability are practically indispensable to the business. Look for key-person situations, also for the business continuation needs of the partnership and close corporation.

Find the contractor's life insurance need and, in submitting your solution, prove that life insurance is efficient, modern and scientific. Give contractor prospects facts, figures, charts and graphs—for this is familiar language to them. Show them that a strong financial program is built from a "blueprint," just like a building, with life insurance providing the foundation and framework and other assets properly integrated for the utmost strength and security.

Credit Executives: See **Accountants.**

Dentists: See **Doctors.**

Department Store Buyers: The department store buyers are intelligent, hardworking, and usually under nervous strain from the pressure of their work. The strain of competition, travel and having to produce profits is such that their big earning years are relatively short.

Buyers are often the breadwinners at home and dependent upon their own incomes for their present and future security. They must necessarily provide for retirement and for protection against immediate loss of their incomes. They come into constant contact with new clothes and home furnishings, thus the temptation to spend too freely is always present. Talk to them about the necessity of providing for tomorrow's needs.

Doctors (Chiropractors, Surgeons, Osteopaths, Dentists): The life value of these professional people is extremely high because of the big investment of time and money in their long years of preparation, and their extraordinary income potential. Point out that their business capital consists of **personal assets:** professional knowledge and skill, and their own two hands. Each day they work is a full day of depreciation, and personal capital can be snuffed out in a moment. Since doctors' capital is destructible, they must have a substantial program of financial security for themselves, and their families. Remember, a deceased doctor's reference books and office equipment are worth very little to family survivors.

Doctors know they cannot look to a paternalistic boss for help in solving these problems. They must rely on **themselves** and provide **their own** security. During their large earning years, they are prone to invest heavily—yet their knowledge of the investment world is usually limited and they haven't the time for investment management. Consequently, they need substantial life insurance and investment programs as well as disability insurance. See **Professionals** in Chapter 2.

Engineers (Civil, Mechanical, Electrical, Chemical, etc.): Engineers, as a rule, have common mental characteristics. They have analytical minds; they are factual and methodical; their reasoning is logical, precise, sequential.

Their job is to solve problems according to scientific formulas, and they are interested in efficiency, shortcuts to an objective, and in new developments.

So you must show them a definite problem and a solution that is factual, logical and scientific. Give them all necessary facts and figures and show them that you are as efficient in solving their financial problems as they are in solving the problems that confront them in their work.

Farmers: They are more than likely to be deliberate individuals and thus resentful of glibness and high pressure. However, they are willing to listen to a reasonable and sincere presentation, but they are usually definite in their own opinions and like to state them. Do not treat these opinions lightly.

Farmers are essentially sole proprietors and a great deal of money is involved in their operations. Don't talk about petty amounts in your insurance illustrations. Farmers are used to paying many thousands of dollars for farm machinery and farm buildings. They can purchase large policies just as easily as professional people can. Talk to them about paying off their mortgages and leaving their farms debt free, educational plans for their children, providing guaranteed income for their widows so that they can hire someone to run the farm, and about balancing inheritances by leaving the farm to the most able child and providing equal values of life insurance for others. Many farmers are very much interested in retirement plans that will enable them to turn the farm over to the children without the necessity of the children having to support them and lodge them for the rest of their lives.

Government Officials (City, County, State, Federal): These officials can be grouped into three classifications: those elected by vote (mayors, aldermen, congressmen, etc.), those appointed (state librarians, state house officials, postmasters, etc.) and Civil Service workers who qualify by examinations and year of service.

Except for Civil Service workers, government officials have uncertain tenures of office. So, the type of life insurance that often interests them most is the high-premium type with substantial cash and loan values to give them something to fall back on if they are removed from office and must find other work. Before seeing these officials, it's wise to gain some knowledge of the retirement and government benefit plans that apply in their cases.

Homemakers: Most wives, and husbands too, do not realize the economic value of a wife who is a full-time homemaker to the family. Should a full-time homemaker die, the month-to-month cost of a housekeeper replacement is staggering. In addition, the husband soon loses his privilege of filing a joint return income tax form, and his taxes go up markedly. Last expense costs are at an all-time high for burial, doctors, nurses, hospital, etc. And in the case of more affluent prospects, estate taxes may be materially increased.

In addition to these reasons for substantial life insurance on the wife are the facts that out of every ten married women, nearly five are working, three out of six mothers with school children are working; and a substantial number of women over 18 have no life insurance. Point out to the husband and wife that her loss would have a strangulating effect on the family budget. Women like insurance policies with appreciable cash accumulation values, and the addition of a family income rider is certainly in order. See pages 67–68.

Lawyers: They are trained, technical and serious individuals. They are known for their thoroughness and attention to detail. They have quick, logical minds and are usually well informed. Most lawyers enjoy arguing for the sake of analysis rather than criticism. Approach lawyers as though they understood your business, for they would resent any implication that they are not versed on the subject. And what they don't understand about your statements, they'll make it their business to find out. Know your points thoroughly so they will not trip you in cross-examination. They will lose confidence in you if you are guilty of misstatements.

As in the case of doctors, the lawyers' skill and knowledge are their greatest capital assets. Such capital is subject to immediate loss and to depreciation throughout the years. This capital needs the protection that only life insurance can give. Also, with an ever-increasing number of law partnerships, there is a fast-growing field for partnership insurance.

Manufacturers: Large manufacturers are often well-to-do with substantial personal, as well as business, assets. They should be approached for life insurance through estate protection and taxation appeals. See the Estate Protection and Business Insurance chapters.

The assets of smaller manufacturers usually represent a large proportion of their worth. The economic well-being of their homes is dependent on that of their businesses. Should they die, their businesses may become definite liabilities to their families. There may be no one capable enough or available to run the business of a deceased owner, and it may have to be liquidated for a ridiculously low figure.

Smaller manufacturers are easier to see than the heads of the large concerns. But they are often thoroughly engrossed in the details of their businesses and they sometimes have difficulty realizing that pouring money into the business is generally no solution to the problems of personal and family security. It must be pointed out that their financial programs usually lack the diversification essential to security and safety. Through life insurance, they should establish separate estates outside of their business estates so that, come what may, their families will have adequate protection. They may be prospects for various business insurance arrangements.

Mechanics: See **Skilled Workers.**

Ministers: Since ministers have a desire to help others which attribute extends to their own loved ones, they usually have a great desire for life insurance protection. But most ministers are not overly paid, so they need special help in setting up plans of security that will do the most for the least amount of outlay. Here is an ideal place for family income policies and riders. However, ministers also need assistance in building extra retirement income to supplement pensions that are frequently far from adequate.

Ministers have a great respect for learning and want their children to have the advantages of higher education. They may be willing to wear the same suit all year, but they want their families to have educational and cultural advantages.

Don't overlook ministers as ideal sources of leads. They know the circumstances of the families in their congregations and they can tell you about births, marriages, new jobs, etc. Stress your desire to serve these people as a financial adviser—just as ministers serve as spiritual advisers. They can appreciate this "partnership" arrangement, and can be most helpful as centers of influence.

Morticians: They need little motivation to buy life insurance, for they are in daily contact with death and the tragic results of death for many families. Morticians also see life insurance in action from day to day, and they are fully convinced of its importance in easing the agonizing fears that beset a family when a parent is taken away.

Besides the usual needs for protection and retirement, morticians often need life insurance as a means of perpetuating their businesses for some member of their own families. In this type of business, the transmission of the business from parent to child is traditional. Also look for partnership insurance needs and key-person situations. And don't overlook the mortician as one of the best centers of influence in a community.

Musicians: See Artists.

Newspaper People (Editors, Writers, Columnists, Correspondents, Cartoonists, Reporters):

Either directly or indirectly, newspaper people come into contact with all conditions and stations of life, from the poverty stricken to the rich, from squalor to luxury, from crookedness and dishonesty to high purpose and great sacrifice. They see fortunes made and lost, and are familiar with the squalid conditions arising from the destruction of income by death or disability. As you talk to them, they may sound hardened to life, but they certainly don't want these misfortunes to befall their loved ones or themselves later in life.

With irregular hours and the tendency to hop from one job to a better one, the newspaper person has a definite need for an adequate life insurance and investment program. Editors and other key personnel in the publishing business are often highly paid. Business insurance, where they own part or all of a business, is essential. Many good publishing houses are dependent upon the extraordinary abilities of a very few people, whose lives should be protected with keyperson insurance.

Nurses: Generally, nurses are dedicated people who work long, hard and irregular hours. Their incomes are usually moderate and more or less fixed at a certain level, unless they become a head nurse, assistant to a prominent doctor, or specialize in some advanced field with greater income possibilities. If they do not work steadily in an institution, their incomes from special assignments may be quite irregular. As in the case of other young people with modest incomes, nurses are keenly desirous of building economic security for their later years. They are especially interested in cash accumulation and retirement plans.

Osteopaths: See **Doctors**.

Pharmacists: In every community and most shopping centers, there is the familiar drugstore which, today, sells everything from tacks to tie racks. Almost every member of every family visits a drugstore once or twice a week, so the pharmacist is a foundation of information about family relationships, ages, conditions of health and family incomes. Thus the pharamacists are not only excellent prospects for personal insurance, they also are ideal, well-posted and valuable centers of influence.

Concentrate on selling **yourself** to pharmacists by serving their life insurance and investment needs completely and intelligently. Then cultivate them as a continual source of qualified leads.

Printers (Owners and Managers of Printing Shops): Printers are manufacturers in that they take paper, ink, and type and produce a finished product. They are retailers to the extent that they must sell their products. The business demands heavy investment in equipment to keep up with the latest printing methods and to offset depreciation.

As in the case of manufacturers or retailers, printers have a tendency to invest money back into the business and to consider that they are thus building security for themselves and their families. It must be pointed out to them that real financial security comes not from putting money into the business, but from getting money **out** of the business so that these funds may be channeled into investments that can never be harmed by failure of the business.

The printers need a favorable credit standing with paper concerns. They need cash values to tide them over dull seasons. They need protection to pay off the contractual business debts. They need insurance to offset the shrinking value of their businesses to their spouses should they die.

Retailers: We are referring here to the small, individual business, not the department store or chain store type of retail business. The small retailers operate largely on credit. They buy on credit, hoping that their customers' flow of money through the cash register will be rapid enough and in such volume as to enable them to pay off debts to their suppliers. They know that their credit is based upon their own character, reputation and ability, and that should they die, their creditors would immediately line up with their hands out.

Here again, we have the problem of divorcing the security of the business from the security of the family. Talk to retailers about family protection independent of the business, diversification, the cleanup of debts, retirement and the various needs for business insurance. Don't overlook the possibility of small group and pension cases. See the **Business Insurance** chapter.

Salespeople: The salesperson is generally the extrovert type; is self-confident, knows how to make a good impression. He or she may rave about the hardships of a sales life, but in reality is optimistic and enthusiastic, or the person couldn't continue in sales.

Money may come easily to the salesperson, but it goes easily, too. He or she wants to dress well and live well, and has a tendency to spend extravagantly. If on commission, salespeople have earnings that fluctuate and they need the sound protection of life insurance.

In talking to salespeople, don't be afraid of too much pressure and enthusiasm on your part. The salesperson respects another salesperson who can give a hardhitting presentation. Stress motivation, use power phrases—appeal to pride, affection, possessive instinct, the maintenance of a high standard of living for their families should they die, and the good things of life for themselves at retirement.

Salespeople are often ambitious to go into business for themselves. Accent the values of life insurance in building cash, as collateral, and as an excellent credit and character reference.

Skilled Workers (Tradespeople, Machinists, Pattern Makers, Die Cutters, Linotype Operators, Compositors, Photoengravers and People in Similar Higher Earning Trades): Skilled workers are proud of their trade. After years of apprenticeship, they think of themselves as skilled personnel. Their wage level is relatively high.

However, their appreciation of life insurance is not likely to have kept pace with their increase in earnings and living standards. So skilled workers generally will need some patient education along this line—but avoid any attitude of condescension! Also avoid hurried noontime or workday interviews. Skilled workers prefer an appointment and the evidence that you have taken time and effort to solve their problems. They understand blueprints, graphs and charts, and because they deal with material things, they like to see something tangible.

In most cases, the spouse must be sold as well as the worker on your proposal. The Social Security approach will interest skilled workers. With some amount of additional life insurance, they can usually turn their Social Security and pension benefits into a complete **income program to protect their families and for their own retirement.** Give them the complete picture! Always keep in mind the skilled worker's pride in the fine things they are now providing for their families.

Store Managers: Store managers are usually under heavy pressure, from above and from below: that is, from management and from the demands of customers. These managers are harassed by countless interruptions and decisions which must be made on the spot, so that interviews during working hours are seldom advisable.

Often store managers' jobs are so frustrating that they are tempted to "get out from under" and start their own businesses. Many do. So talk to them about a sinking fund—for their families if they should die or for themselves if they need money quickly for a business opportunity. Of course, as they visualize the strain of their work over the years ahead, retirement income is an appealing subject, also.

Present a definite, well-ordered plan for them. They are systematic in their thinking and, given the necessary facts, they can make decisions in a hurry. Also be on the lookout for store managers who are part-owners, or managers who can be classified as key persons. Here again are opportunities for business insurance interviews.

Store Owners: See **Retailers.**

Students: Of course it is difficult to put the attitudes and thought processes of students into particular categories. They come from all kinds of environments and their financial situations are dissimilar.

Those students who are working part time and helping to pay their college expenses are good prospects for life insurance. They are conscientious and will want to have any tuition loans or advances paid off in case they die. Term insurance is often advisable, with the object of converting to permanent insurance later.

Students who are not working may not be immediate prospects. Their **parents** may be, however, and they may consider insurance on their children's lives if tuition money has been borrowed from a lending institution or life insurance cash values or family reserves. Four years spent in college is a heavy drain on family finances and, should the student not live, the wasted cost of the education will prove a substantial loss. Students who are taking special training requiring additional years of preparation to become doctors, professors, technical specialists, etc., should especially be protected because of the exceptionally heavy investment in their schooling.

Teachers (University, College, High School, Elementary School): Teachers' salaries are within well-defined limits. As they look ahead, they see these limits and are often tempted into speculative investments. Teachers need life insurance to protect them from investment errors that might wreck rather than expand their savings.

Teachers are especially anxious that their children have the finest educational opportunities. Retirement, too, is a concern that is uppermost in their minds.

But, of course, they need life insurance for all of the usual reasons: last expenses, mortgage cancellation, family income, etc. Talk safety. Show them that life insurance is the modern method of achieving financial success, without risk, without doubt, and without the worry of money management.

Unmarried teachers are greatly interested in the accumulation of cash values for special purposes as well as for security in retirement. Many are fascinated by the thought of having enough money someday for extensive traveling.

BEST TIME TO SEE

Accountants—any month after April.
Business Executives—after 10:30 A.M.
Chemists—4 to 5 P.M.
Clergy members—any time after Tuesday.
Contractors—before 9 A.M.; after 5 P.M.
Dentists—before 9:30 A.M.
Engineers—4 to 5 P.M.
Homemakers—11 A.M. to Noon; 2 to 4 P.M.
Lawyers—11 A.M. to 2 P.M.
Pharmacists—1 to 3 P.M.
Publishers and Printers—after 3 P.M.
Retailers—before 9 A.M.; 1 to 2:30 P.M.
Teachers—7:30 to 9 P.M.

2

Tested Sales Ideas

Everyone you call on has a need. or a number of needs, for life insurance, depending on his or her life situation. This section provides you with strong reasons why life insurance is the ideal answer to your client's needs, whether they be for:

Last Expenses
Mortgage Cancellation
Emergency Funds
Educational Funds
Adjustment Income
Family Income
Widow's or Widower's Income

> Don't let today's solution turn into tomorrow's problem—*anon.*

Retirement Income
Juvenile Protection
Annuity Income
Sickness and Accident

Here are hundreds of compelling ideas and phrases for arousing interest, provoking thought, revealing needs. maintaining interest—for all classes of prospects.

FAMILY SECURITY

While no two families have identical problems upon the death of a parent, all families have these general needs: **cash** requirements and **income** requirements.

CASH REQUIREMENTS

Immediate Cash Requirements

1. **A fund for final expenses:** Hospital, medical and funeral expenses; normal household bills and

installment obligations; the cost of administering and probating the estate—these are the expenses that must be paid first before a spouse and children are entitled to the residue of the deceased spouse's estate.

2. **A permanent home fund:** This is a fund to write off the mortgage so the family can keep the home. If the family is not now living in a home that is being purchased, it can be a special fund to serve as a substantial down payment on a permanent home.

Later Cash Requirements

1. **An emergency fund:** A cushion against the shock of unexpected bills that cannot be absorbed by regular income: major illnesses and accidents, home repairs, car repairs, etc.
2. **Educational funds:** While not as essential as other funds, as many dollars as possible should be set aside for the higher education or special training so essential today in preparing a child for a business or profession in our competitive economy.

INCOME REQUIREMENTS

Immediate Income Requirements

1. **Adjustment income:** This acts as a "stair step" that reduces gradually, enabling the family to step down gracefully to a lower level of income.
2. **Dependency period income:** This is the single, most important area of family planning. An adequate monthly income is needed to keep the family and home together while the children are young and dependent, and while they need their mother or father's care and attention during their formative years.

Later Income Requirements

1. **Life income for the spouse:** An income that is needed during the Blackout Period when no Social Security income is paid from the time the youngest child is age 18 until the spouse's retirement income starts, and on into his or her later years to prevent the spouse from becoming a burden to the children while they are getting started in life.
2. **Retirement income:** A guaranteed, lifelong income provided from dollars that are accumulated over a period of years. In view of the tendency of business to require workers to retire at 65, or even

earlier, this income is essential if Mom and Dad are to be independent of the children and of social welfare. With the percentage of older people in the population increasing steadily, the problem of retirement income will become more pressing and necessitate careful planning in early years.

LAST EXPENSES

A few years ago a last expense fund of $5,000 to $10,000 was considered adequate. Now medical bills, alone, may double or triple those amounts.

Doctors' bills are inflated because the bills they pay are higher; hospital bills are staggering because of increased operational expenses; the lawyer, the undertaker, and all other creditors pass along bills that reflect their increased costs of living—and the parent who dies has no one to pass them on to except the family. With higher taxes and court costs, the accumulated burden is enough to crack the foundation of a person's plans for family security.

It must be pointed out to married couples that if there is no ready cash to pay these debts, the family will suffer great hardship. Either the money will be squeezed out of funds intended for family income—or possibly out of a spouse's paycheck, if he or she must go to work to keep the creditors away from the front door. It is obvious that life insurance is the best property for the job—a big job—because it can furnish ample funds at the exact moment they are needed.

Dying automatically creates added expenses and only life insurance can automatically create the money to pay those expenses.

LAST EXPENSE QUOTES

Are you trying to do today's last expense job **with yesterday's last expense fund**?

" "

The bills that come due because of your death are **your** bills. Somebody has to pay them. Can your spouse and children do it better than you?

" "

Life insurance provides funds **for** the estate rather than **from** the estate.

" "

Life insurance prevents freezing current dollars in a last expense fund for which there is no use today. Instead, you can buy more things today with the dollars left over after the relatively small insurance premium is paid. When the last expense fund is needed tomorrow, it will be there.

" "

Even on estates between $10,000 and $50,000, 18 percent is absorbed by funeral costs alone—**$1 out of $5 of the family's capital!**

" "

If you had to raise $10,000 or $15,000 in cash today, **would it be an easy job?** Would it be any easier for your spouse? Wouldn't it be better to set aside a few dollars a month now rather than put the burden on his (or her) shoulders later?

" "

A special last-expense policy prevents **sacrifice of valuable estate assets** that would otherwise have to be sold at a loss to meet the cost of death.

MORTGAGE CANCELLATION

Most "homeowners" actually do not own their homes, but are buying them on a long-term installment plan. However, no one these days is ashamed of a mortgaged home. A mortgage is customary and commonplace, and most persons have no hesitancy in talking about it.

A mortgage is really a blessing to the family, **so long as the homeowner is here to keep up the payments.** Without the mortgage arrangement, it

> You wanted your family to have this home or you would not have bought it. What assurance have you now that they will get to keep it?

would be just about impossible to make a start on buying a home; with it, a person can have all the joys and pride of home ownership and pay for the home while the family is living in it. So the home, even a mortgaged home, is one of the homeowner's **finest assets** while he or she is alive.

BUT if the owner's not here to keep up the mortgage payments, the home actually may become a **liability** to the surviving spouse and children. They inherit not only the debt of the mortgage principal, but also thousands of dollars of future, unpaid interest **unless** a mortgage cancellation policy stamps the mortgage "PAID" and lets the family enjoy the same neighborhood environment, the same schools, the same church, the same neighborly friends that the homeowner and spouse selected together.

Just as the home can be one of a couple's finest assets, a mortgage cancellation policy can be one of the most vital features of family security.

MORTGAGE QUOTES

Is it easier for you to raise a 2 percent premium on your mortgage **or for your spouse to raise 100 percent of the balance due at your death?**

Do you really want your spouse to be forced to write checks for the next 20 years, checks totalling thousands of dollars in future interest added on to the principal you originally borrowed? (For calculating specific examples, check the mortgage tables beginning on page 282). This mortgage cancellation policy not only writes off the mortgage principal, but all of the future interest as well. That's why this is one of the finest bargains in insurance.

You wouldn't think of living in your home half an hour without fire insurance. But loss of the home through your death is a far greater hazard, as these figures show:

Deaths Per Thousand At Selected Ages

Age	*Occurrence of Death*
25	1.77
35	2.11
45	4.55
55	10.47

Mr. (or Ms.) Homeowner, when you bought your home, did the mortgage company give you a choice between a cancellable and a non-cancellable mortgage? . . . **What I mean by that is whether they offered you a mortgage on which the payments will have to be completed no matter what happens to you, or one where in case something should happen to you, they'd cancel all payments still due and turn the title over to your spouse immediately.**

If you didn't get a cancellable mortgage, I'd like to show you how to convert the one you have into such a contract.

" "

Mr. (or Ms.) Homeowner, I'm sure you don't think more of your mortgage lender than you do of your own family.

Yet, according to your present home-purchase arrangements, the mortgage holder comes first. THE LENDER CAN'T LOSE. If your house burns down, the fire insurance company pays the lender; if your house payments stop, the mortgage lender can take away the home.

So, your family stands to lose everything—the home and thousands of dollars you've put into it—if you're not here to meet the mortgage payments.

But with mortgage insurance, you put the family first. THEY CAN'T LOSE. Instead, they gain a debt-free home. You do want your family to come first, don't you, Mr. (or Ms.) Homeowner?

EMERGENCY AND OPPORTUNITY FUNDS

Every family/couple knows about the "rough spots" in life that tend to disrupt the budget. The car breaks down—one of the children needs orthodontic

> Objections to buying life insurance sound so convincing—until they echo in a widow's memory.

braces—the plumbing gets out of kilter—and heaven knows what will happen next!

Money also is required to take advantage of opportunities, such as getting started in a new business or making any kind of personal investment. No one can anticipate the frequency or the severity of these financial setbacks or when opportunity may knock, so it is impractical to establish a level of family income that will take care of emergency bills and investment opportunities as they arise.

For these reasons it is logical for a couple to **create a special reserve fund for family emergencies and opportunities**. Also, with this nest egg to fall back on, the widow, for example, does not have to go into debt when the inevitable emergencies strike. She wouldn't have to go out and find a job to get extra money during these crucial times.

Once again, **life insurance is the ideal source of these extra funds**. Emphasize the advisability of an additional policy of $10,000, $20,000 or more to meet this urgent need.

QUOTES

Mr. (or Ms.) Prospect, it's difficult for you to decide what level of monthly income your family will need, so long as there are disturbing questions in your mind—"What if **this** should happen—and what if **that** should happen?" Why don't we set up a special emergency fund and then we can assume that all the other monthly bills will be fairly regular?

" "

Mr. (or Ms.) Prospect, all of us fight to have a little something in reserve—in the bank—in savings bonds—or in life insurance cash values—just in case some emergency or opportunity might come along. Did you ever consider that even if you are not here, financial emergencies will **always** be around, so far as your family is concerned? **That's why it's so important to set up this special fund.**

" "

You know, Mr. (or Ms.) Prospect, I'm always saying that maybe **next** month will be smooth sailing. But then something almost inevitably happens to disrupt the budget—the roof leaks, or one of the youngsters falls down and breaks an arm, and so it goes. Then I hope for the next month after that. But it's usually the same story over again. I imagine you have a similar problem with your budget, don't you? Emergencies are just facts of life, and, since life will go on for our families even though we are not here it would be smart to set up a special fund for such emergencies .

EDUCATIONAL FUNDS

The importance of advanced education or special training for children is becoming increasingly apparent to parents. Surveys show that young people without higher education are under a severe disadvantage in today's competitive world.

Today, more than ever before, an education or special training is the **greatest gift** parents can give to children. Today's children will face the world of tomorrow—a world vastly different from that in which parents began their careers.

Tomorrow will continue to be be a world of specialization, of polished skills, of technology in business and industry. Tomorrow's standard equipment will be an advanced education—tomorrow's competition for jobs will be among highly trained men and women. **Tomorrow's chances for the untrained will be only the jobs no one wants—the jobs without a future.**

Is there any finer investment a parent can make in the child's future than a life insurance policy to guarantee a college education or other special training?

COLLEGE QUOTES

If you aren't here to pay your child's college bills, who would you rather have pay those bills for you—**my company or your child?**

" "

For every genius stimulated by an attic, hundreds of thousands have been dulled beyond usefulness.

" "

A life insurance policy is **the greatest gift in the world** to the greatest girl or boy in the world—from the greatest Dad and Mom in the world.

" "

For your children, educational insurance means "parents who loved us." Can money buy more than this?

" "

Mr. and Mrs. Prospect, you expect to send Bill to college if you are able. But some parents will never live to see their sons reach college age. Unless you do something about this risk, you are playing Russian roulette with Bill's future.

" "

Mr. and Mrs. Prospect, about 17 years from now, in September, your son is going out to the airport with several of his high school buddies. He is either going to college with them, or he is going to see them off to college.

If you were in your boy's shoes and he were in your shoes, **what decision would you want him to make about this plan?**

" "

Mr. and Mrs. Prospect, if a big company said to you, "We will guarantee your child a college education worth an estimated $250,000, and all you need to do is save $5 a week," **would you look over the plan?**

" "

In arranging funds for your child's college education, you have three choices:

CHOICE 1—Wait until your child enters college, then pay college expenses out of your income.
BUT—**would it be possible to take $8,000 or $5,000 or even $2,000 out of a year's income?** And what if your income stops because you are no longer here to bring it home?
CHOICE 2—Start now and put some money aside each year in bank savings plans.
BUT—**haven't you found that it's so easy to skip deposits or to spend what has been saved?** And what will protect a long-term savings plan against the ever-present hazard of disability or death?
CHOICE 3—Create an **insured college fund today!** (Outline the guaranteed benefits of the educational insurance plan.)

Annual Education Funding for Newborn Child at 8% after tax (in round numbers)

(1) Top Rated "Ivy League" type school	$ 7,000
(2) State University	1,800
(3) Mid-Range	6,000

Lump-Sum Funding

1. $70,000
2. 18,000
3. 58,000

Annual Funding for a Nine-Year-Old Child

1. $10,000
2. 8,500
3. 2,500

Lump-Sum Funding

1. $76,000
2. 64,000
3. 20,000

Educational Costs Future First Year of College

Newborn Child	$50,000
Age 2	44,000
4	38,000
6	34,000
8	30,000
10	25,000
12	22,500
14	19,600
16	17,000

ADJUSTMENT INCOME

When a parent dies, the shock to the family's standard of living may be quite severe during the first few years after death. If a parent is bringing home $2,000 or $4,000 a month, you can imagine how painfully the family will be jolted by an **overnight drop in income** to, say, $1,000 or $1,500 a month. The family's budget would have to be slashed drastically all along the line.

Given time, the family can make the necessary adjustment to a substantial cut in income. What they need **is a gradually declining income,** enabling them to make successive reductions in the family budget over a three-, four- or five-year period.

The adjustment income need offers many opportunities for additional sales of good-sized blocks of extra life insurance. Such policies can be sold on either a package or total needs basis. An adjustment income sale is especially convenient since the existing program **need not be disturbed in any way.** The adjustment income is simply illustrated as an essential "topping" for the present program.

On the next page is a handy table showing the **approximate** amounts of insurance required for successive levels of monthly adjustment income. Also shown are examples of typical income patterns and the approximate amounts of life insurance required.

ADJUSTMENT INCOME TABLE

Extra Income Desired	*For 1st Year*	*Add for 2nd Year*	*Add for 3rd Year*	*Add for 4th Year*
$100	$1,190	$1,160	$1,130	$1,100
150	1,700	1,740	1,690	1,650
200	2,370	2,310	2,260	2,200
250	2,970	2,890	2,820	2,760
300	3,560	3,470	3,390	3,300

Example of monthly adjustment income pattern, using the above table:

Need $300 for one year	$ 3,560
Then $250 for one year	2,970
Then $200 for the next two years	2,260
	2,200
Total	$10,990

ADJUSTMENT QUOTES

Suppose your family lived in a second floor apartment and it catches on fire. They'd rush for the stairs, of course. But what if there were no stairs? They'd have to jump, and **there would be great danger of their getting hurt.**

Similarly, your family is living well on the income you are now bringing home. But if your life is cut short and that income stops, there would be a big drop to a lower income level. If your family must jump quickly from the higher to the lower level, they are going to be hurt badly. But if you provide stairs, they can walk down and not get hurt.

" "

A big reason for setting up blood banks is to help patients overcome shock. If an accident victim gets over the shock of the first few days, he or she has a good chance of recovering. Someday your family may face the shock of dropping to a much lower income level. If they can get by for a few years, they'll be all right. **Why not give them a "dollar bank" to help them through that period?**

" "

Does a child stop wanting ice cream cones the moment Mom or Dad dies? Or stop yearning for a bicycle. Or stop longing for a new outfit? Plan for the "little extras" in children's lives—**a little extra life insurance makes life worth living.**

FAMILY INCOME

Probably the most vital part of a family program of security is adequate income during the **Dependency Period**. These are the years from the time a parent dies until the youngest child is beginning to earn his or her own way. And these are the years when responsibili-

> Do you know of any other plan which will enable you to will your family thousands of dollars before you have earned them?

ties and financial burdens lie heaviest upon the surviving spouse—the years when she or he must keep the home together, clothe, feed, train and educate the children. These are the years when family living expenses are at their peak. These are the years during which the children's characters and habits are formed. **These are indeed the critical years!**

The need for a dependable family income during the dependency period is obvious to everyone. And in view of today's living costs, it is essential that parents think in terms of adequate income. With the help of increased Social Security benefits, a father, for example, no longer needs to ask himself, "If something should happen to me, how little could they get along on?" No longer need he expect the family to suffer great hardships in order to keep the family circle intact. In helping parents set up family income programs, avoid basing the plans on **minimums**. Instead, help parents to raise their sights and to think in terms of income that will enable the family to live on a **comfortable basis—to live as they would want**

their spouse and children to live, just as though they were here to provide for them themselves.

WIDOW'S INCOME

Many husbands are complacent in the thought that a few thousand dollars will see his widow through after the children are grown. This is hardly a practical thought if she has been a full-time homemaker and has given years of her life to holding the home together and caring for the children. **And it's hardly a realistic thought in view of today's living costs.**

Let us consider just three items in the widow's budget: food, clothing and shelter without totaling any of the desirable extras that make life really worth living. And to cut these requirements down to a minimum, let's suppose a widow has a home that's all paid for and needs only a nominal amount of household expenses and upkeep.

Of course it won't be enough, but assume the widow can get by on $80 a month for essential clothing and other items of personal care. And skimpy as the amount sounds, suppose we allow her **$300 a month for household expenses**—light, heating, gas, water, telephone, real estate taxes, repairs and replacements, etc. Finally, let's hold the **food budget to $10 a day,** although she would likely go hungry on that.

Considering just these three items, see below what they would amount to in terms of dollar needs for 10, 15 and 20 years after the youngest child has left home and Mom is all alone.

The Widow's Needs

Considering just $80 a month for clothes, $300 a month for household expenses and $10 a day for food, look at the total income a widow would need over the years:

Number of Years	*Clothes*	*Household*	*Food*	*Total*
10	$ 9,600	$36,000	$36,500	$ 82,100
15	14,400	54,000	54,750	123,150
20	19,200	72,000	73,000	164,200

Figures like these will awaken a husband to the vital need of providing sufficient funds for the widow later in life. He can't remain complacent in the face of a need for $100,000 or $150,000, just to insure the bare necessities of life.

If the husband doesn't furnish the necessary money, where will it come from? If she tries to work she might have a difficult time finding a decent job and holding it. If she can't work, she might live with the children—if anyone has room for her—if she can force herself to disrupt the privacy and normal home life of the children. And if she refused to burden the children, what then? **The only solution is life insurance for lifelong income.**

FAMILY INCOME QUOTES

Suppose you didn't get paid this month or next month or for several months. How would you get along? Would it be any easier for your widow and children if your salary **never** came in again?

" "

It would be a wonderful thing if you could leave in a dresser drawer at home a checkbook in which you had written checks for $1,000 or more a month for every month your wife might live after your death. But you might not leave a large enough bank balance to honor them all. Why don't you open an account at the life insurance bank where, no matter when you die, **your balance will be large enough to honor all checks?** It can never be overdrawn.

" "

At no time in life is a widow less able to become a breadwinner than when she first becomes a widow.

" "

Most men support two families—the one they live with now, and the one they will leave at their deaths.

" "

Death of income is the death that life insurance is primarily concerned with.

" "

Do you know of any other plan that permits you to will to your family thousands of dollars before you have earned them?

ADVANTAGES OF MONTHLY INCOME FROM LIFE INSURANCE

Safety of Principal and Income: There are no investment losses, funds are guaranteed by entire assets of the company, rate of interests are guaranteed and future payments guaranteed by contract.

An Ideal Will: There are no court costs, no attorney's fees, no administrator's expenses, no trustee's commissions, no red tape, no publicity and no delays. Even on an estate of $10,000, a 10 percent administration cost equals $1,000!

Income Regular: Income starts immediately—no fluctuations as result of business recessions, absolutely the safest form of providing future income from an estate.

Benefits Safeguarded: Funds cannot be stolen, assigned, hypothecated or lost through unfortunate investments or unwise loans.

Definite Monthly Income: Regular monthly income enables family to adjust living costs and standards to those required.

You Are Trustee of Own Estate: Not your brother-in-law—or a lawyer—or a relative, but you yourself can plan exactly how you want your estate distributed. Under options, your life insurance estate becomes a preinvested estate.

RETIREMENT QUOTES

For a fuller treatment of retirement, *see* Chapter 10.

Years do not make fortunes but they do make us old men and old women. Someday you'll get your last paycheck. What plan do you have to take the place of it?

" "

Mr. (or Ms.) Prospect, it used to be that only a rich person could afford to think about retiring on an income. But now it's different. With Social Security, a topping of retirement income from a moderate amount of life insurance and a good investment plan,

almost any person can look forward to a comfortable old age. Let me show you what I mean.

" "

The life insurance retirement income plan is unselfish. It does not deny your family protection now in order to give you funds for your old age. It **covers both needs.** Is there any other plan on earth that can do this?

" "

Mr. Prospect, look in a mirror and tell me what you see. Sure you see youth, earning ability, ambition, energy and all that goes with a healthy young man. **Now look in the mirror and imagine it is 30 to 35 years from now.** What do you see? Same fellow. Hair may be gray or thin, a few lines and wrinkles. Youth gone, not as much energy.

Mr. Prospect, tell me who is the old fellow's best friend? Who on this earth can do more for him than anyone else? Isn't it the young man looking in the mirror at him right now? **Isn't it your job to take care of that old man—and not your children's job?**

LET'S TAKE A LOOK AT YOUR PROGRAM

It is surprising how quickly yesterday's well-planned life insurance program can become obsolete.

> The amount of life insurance you own is the price you have put on your future—your measure of your value to your family. Are you satisfied with your price tag?

Here is a list of factors that tend to make a program outdated:

1. **Lack of Flexibility:** This can happen when the program provides levels of fixed monthly income that the family is powerless to change during inflationary periods. Also evident when the widow is too restricted in her right to withdraw sufficient principal to meet serious family emergencies.
2. **Changes in Family Status:** The names of additional children must be added as secondary beneficiaries. It also may be necessary to shift more income to the dependency period to allow for newly born children. Beneficiary changes are needed when previously named beneficiaries no longer exist or when there is no longer a need or desire to have them participate in the proceeds.

   Unusual situations may also require changes, such as additional proceeds needed for a disabled child, or a redistribution of proceeds to give younger children adequate income over necessarily longer periods. (In case both parents die.)

3. **Social Security Changes:** In recent years there have been major changes every year. Changes in benefit levels and eligibility requirements have a vital effect on the life insurance program and must be taken into consideration in revising the program.
4. **New Tax Laws:** Among the more important recent laws are those dealing with income tax advantages of proceeds paid to the widow, and estate tax advantages. Certain actions must be taken to benefit from these advantages.
5. **New Employee Benefits:** Programs must be modified to accommodate additional or new group insurance, profit-sharing benefits, pension plans, etc.
6. **Policy Provisions:** A check should be made to see that policies contain certain beneficial clauses as automatic premium loan, spendthrift clause, common disaster provision, etc. Also every effort should be made to remove or reduce policy restrictions.
7. **Adequacy:** This is the most important reason for a review of the program. **Is there enough life insurance to do the job expected of it,** in view of higher living costs and living standards?

LEAD QUESTIONS IN TOTAL NEEDS SELLING

1. **Have you** made the proceeds of your policies **judgment proof** against the claims of creditors of your spouse and children?
2. **Have you** included the **common disaster** and **spendthrift clauses** in your insurance?
3. **Have you** disinherited any children by failing to check beneficiaries?
4. **Have you** determined **how much monthly income** your insurance will pay your family and for how long?; also the **pension power** of your life insurance?
5. **Have you** set up your insurance so as to eliminate **needless taxes and unnecessary administration costs?**
6. Have you considered **whose side of the family** will get the insurance if you and your wife meet with a fatal accident?
7. **Have you** dealt fairly with **younger children in** the distribution of your life insurance?
8. **Have you** taken advantage of the **marital deduction** to reduce your estate taxes?
9. **Have you** rearranged your **settlement options** to make them fit in with recent Social Security changes?

> It's not what you say so much as how you say it—*Ben Feldman*

10. **Have you** arranged beneficiary plans to make the proceeds free of as much **federal income tax** as possible, with all the savings that such arrangements may mean to your wife?

THE FARMER IS "BIG BUSINESS"

The needs of a family for life insurance are universal, whether the family lives in the city or in the country. But farmers' needs are especially urgent because they're "sole proprietors" of enterprises that are **big business** by all standards of measurement.

As a self-employed farm operator, the farmer has a large capital investment in land, buildings, farm machinery and possibly livestock. The amount of income that he or she enjoys is based almost entirely upon **ability;** upon the way that he or she manages investments. True, capital has a certain value. But that value is responsible for only a part of the farmer's total income. **A large portion comes from the ability to make the investment produce.**

If the farmer dies, his management and work skills are lost to the family along with a substantial portion of the income. Some methods of replacement must be found.

QUOTES FOR FARMERS

Hired Hand Money: Mr. Farmer, suppose today you were taken sick or injured so that you couldn't do your regular farm work. Of course, your neighbors would step in and help for a few days, but if you were to die, your wife would have to hire someone to do the work. That would take money, wouldn't it? And the chances are that a hired hand couldn't make the farm pay like you can. Life insurance can provide the hired hand's salary and prevent shrinkage of farm income.

" "

Your Will: Mr. Farmer, have you made (or revised) your will to make sure that your estate goes exactly where you want it to?

For instance, if you were to die without a will, it might take months—years—for the courts to get things straightened out. You can imagine how the farm would become run down. Then they'd split it up between your wife and children. I'm sure you wouldn't want to tie everyone's hands, have the farm ruined and then have it cut up into small sections. With the right kind of will the farm can be given intact to one heir with life insurance providing equal bequests to others. For a farmer with a substantial estate, the marital deduction may save thousands of dollars in death taxes!

" "

Your Son: Mr. Farmer, how would you like to say to that boy of yours on your 60th or 65th birthday:

"Son, I am going to give you the farm today. I'm not going to sell it to you. I won't ask you to farm it on shares. I don't want you to wait until I'm dead. I want to give it to you right now, equipment, livestock, the new crop—everything. And I don't want you to have to take care of Mom and me.

"Son, I can do it because my life insurance is going to pay me and your mother a nice income as long as we live. You take the farm right now."

" "

The Alternatives Your Widow Would Face: (a) She could **operate the farm herself.** BUT—farming is hard work. And she'd have to face big decisions wherein an error in judgment might spell failure. (b) She could **hire a hand to help run the farm.** BUT—good hands are hard to get. A hired man doesn't have your know-how, your incentive. He doesn't have much at stake. The farm's income is almost bound to drop off—and his wages will reduce it still further. (c)

She could rent the farm on shares. BUT—she'd have only one-half or less of the income from the farm. And no renter will have your personal interest in the farm or be able to make it pay like you do. (d) She could **rent the farm for cash.** BUT—she'd lose her home. And it's hardly likely that the meager rental could take care of even the most basic family needs. (e) Or she could **sell the farm.** BUT—forced sales bring low prices. She'd be sacrificing years of effort—yours and hers—plus all future income from the farm. THE BEST SOLUTION IS GUARANTEED INCOME FROM LIFE INSURANCE!

MR. FARMER, HOW ABOUT YOUR SOCIAL SECURITY?

Of course this subject of Social Security could get rather complicated. But you can keep it simple by asking the **three big questions** that seem to be in every farmer's mind:

"How much retirement will it pay me and how much income will it pay my family?"

"How much do I have to pay for it, and how do I go about paying it?"

"What do I have to do to make SURE we get all the benefits that are coming to us?

So if you have just a few minutes, let's start with the first question.

(You should carry with you at all times an up-to-date table of Social Security benefits for reference purposes. Such figures are contained in Dearborn•R&R Newkirk's yearly *Pocket Tables*.)

LIFE INSURANCE FOR A SON OR DAUGHTER

Here are the benefits to buying a life insurance policy for a son or daughter:

1. **Buying** a policy for your boy or girl early in life guarantees a low premium rate.
2. **It** protects insurability—guarantees that there will be at least one policy.
3. It is an excellent employment and business reference.
4. **It** helps avoid customary first investment losses.
5. **It** teaches the lesson of systematic thrift, an especially important point because many young people fail on account of inability to save.
6. **It** builds character, persistency, regularity in meeting obligations.
7. **It** provides cash values for college or for a business start or home purchase.
8. **It** creates a sense of joint responsibility toward you and the mother.

9. **It** teaches respect for conservative investment and unquestioned stability and leads away from speculation and risk.
10. **It** is the first step in creating an estate that becomes increasingly valuable year by year, providing cash values, protection and retirement income in the same contract.

BUY THIS PLAN FOR YOUR CHILD

Not because you expect your child to die.

Not because you have invested considerable money in raising him or her.

Not because he or she has anyone dependent upon him or her today.

Not because he or she will understand the great value of a policy.

BUT

Because when he or she grows to adulthood you want him or her to be a good citizen and a successful businessperson.

Because the foundation upon which successful businesspersons build is good character and habits of thrift.

Because if your child marries he or she will need life insurance for family protection.

Because it will cost less to start now.

Because the policy will be paid up at the time that most adults start paying.

Because it creates a fund that will help to make your child independent in old age.

Because your child is probably insurable now.

Because you wish that your parents had taken out such a policy for you when you were a child.

YOUR CHILD'S PROBLEM

With taxes heavy and after-tax investment yields cut accordingly, is there a plan that will help your youngster solve the dilemma of winning financial success? YES! TIME AND A LIFE INSURANCE PLAN can solve the problem. How?

Assume you have a child age ten now and he or she waits until later in life to start accumulating $30,000 principal needed, at 4 percent **net after taxes,** to produce $100 a month interest income, starting at age 65. How much will he have to save each year from age 25, 30 or 35 to age 65, to produce the principal needed? At 4% net, he must save:

Age 25	$301 yearly	$12,040 total
Age 30	387 yearly	13,545 total
Age 35	506 yearly	15,180 total

But by starting early in life and using the life insurance way of creating income, your child can have the following monthly incomes at age 65 by depositing these nominal sums each year, as well as an increasing face amount of life insurance at retirement age.

Age	*Yearly Deposit*	*Age 65 Cash Value (Div. Included)*	*Insurance Face Amount at 65*	*Monthly Life Income at 65 (10 yr. cc)*
10	$238	$161,401	$267,165	$1,305.73
15	278	125,707	207,972	1,016.91
20	322	99,623	164,716	805.95

Based on a participating Life Paid up at 65 contract with an initial face amount of $25,000. This is a good way of helping your child meet the problem of creating life income in the face of after-tax investment yields.

THE ANNUITY SOLVES THE PROBLEM!

THE PROBLEM

MANY OLDER PEOPLE . . . have a limited amount of capital, which must provide income for the rest of their lives.

BUT IF THEY . . .start using up their principal, they may outlive these funds and have no money in later life.

IS THERE A WAY TO GET ADEQUATE INCOME FROM LIMITED CAPITAL?

THE SOLUTION

Use the Annuity

At age 60, $75,280 invested in an annuity . . . can produce $6,000 annual lifetime income (Male 10 yr. cc., or even more with other options).

At age 65, $70,560 invested in an annuity . . . can produce $6,000 annual lifetime income (Male 10 yr. cc., or even more with other options).

MORE FOR LESS

Under the interest-capital plan, capital dare not be invaded if **life income** is to be maintained. But the annuity plan may provide a far larger income and guarantee it for life. Ideal for the older person with limited capital!

ANNUITY QUOTES

An annuity provides the only way in the entire realm of finance that you can spend your own money during your lifetime, certain that it will last **as long as you live.**

" "

You have enough financial problems; why not buy an annuity and rid yourself of all financial worries forever?

" "

Corporate bonds may depreciate; stocks and real estate need watching—no assured income. **The annuity has none of these disadvantages.** Where can you put your money to better advantage?

" "

Men and women of wealth are large buyers of annuities; **they know value.**

" "

An annuity provides a definite assurance of **maximum income** and **peace of mind** that cannot be had from any other type of investment.

" "

When you fill out your income tax report, the **tax savings** on your annuity will gladden your heart. Then you will appreciate doubly what a magnificent investment it is.

" "

When you own an annuity, you have everything to gain and nothing to lose; the **longer you live, the more you get.**

" "

The annuity will convert **limited capital into a liberal, lifetime, guaranteed income.**

PROFESSIONALS

Professional people need a **much higher ratio** of life insurance, on a comparable income basis, than farmers, merchants or manufacturers, to offset the business property values those in the latter groups accumulate as a part of their estates. Those property assets can go on producing income for farmers, merchants or manufacturers, even if they are disabled, or for their families, if they die.

But the skill and reputation of professional people **can be turned into income for themselves or their loved ones only so long as they are able to work.** At death, their professional skill is destroyed instantly. When they retire, their professional skill produces no further income.

Professional people should make sure that they have a clear understanding of these points:

1. When a business person, farmer, merchant or manufacturer dies, his or her family has the farm or business assets to fall back on, but
2. When the professional person dies, his or her effects go on the market as used office furniture, books or secondhand office instruments with little value for the family.
3. The professional people need (a) adequate family protection, (b) retirement income, (c) partnership insurance, if in association with other professional partners, (d) a policy equal to accounts outstanding, if they are to be protected fairly and (e) for investment, they need discounted or single premium plans.
4. Disability or physical impairment such as loss of an eye or loss of a hand can almost instantly wreck the future income earning power of many professional people. Where a store or shopkeeper could continue in business, in most cases, in event of such losses, the physician or surgeon, dentist or attorney, and so on, would be compelled to seek other work.
5. The life insurance plan, with its waiver of premium provision in case of disability, is the only financial plan the professional person can use to make sure physical impairment will not destroy his or her cash accumulations and family protection programs.

QUOTES FOR PROFESSIONALS

Doctor, have you ever given consideration to the tremendous investment you have in the ability you bring to your job? Given enough time, you can make that investment pay off handsomely. **Why not underwrite that time?**

" "

Doctor, if a man were dangerously ill and called you, **he'd want the best treatment you could give him**, regardless of cost. Shouldn't the same be true when a person is in financial ill health and seriously in need of professional help?

" "

If I had a legal problem, Mr. (or Ms.) Attorney, you would expect me to go to a lawyer and get professional advice. You have a life insurance problem. **Which is better?** For you to decide what kind and how much life insurance you want or for you to refer your problem to someone with training and experience as a life underwriter?

" "

Mr. Engineer, you know that in building a bridge across a river it must be long enough—and strong enough to last a long time. In constructing a life insurance program you bridge a good many years. It must be **long enough** and **strong enough** and **safe enough** to serve its purpose.

QUOTES FOR THE WEALTHY

Life insurance enables you to take funds off the top of your estate, where it will be subject to heavy estate taxes, and to transfer part of the assets to other members of your family who are in lower income tax brackets, thus effecting both estate and income tax savings.

" "

One bad series of investments at the end of a lifetime of good investments can tear down your whole program.

" "

Life insurance enables you to put surplus funds into an investment that will not yield current income, subject to high taxes when added to earned income.

" "

Men and women of wealth have purchased life insurance property in such amounts that companies had to restrict the sums they they would accept from individual families. The action of the shrewdest investors in the country is reason enough for men and women of wealth to look into this plan with utmost care, to have their attorneys and accountants give their opinion on its soundness and value.

Investment: Farsighted men and women of wealth diversify investments so that the chances of loss are lessened. Your heirs may not be able to invest as wisely as you, so the property is apt to depreciate after your death; but that part of your funds placed in life insurance will **never depreciate**; it will provide liberal, lifetime, management-free income.

Gift Tax Benefit: Life insurance and annuities represent an ideal investment to use in exercising your money-saving gift tax deductions.

Estate Transfer Taxes: Though the federal estate tax laws have been liberalized, estate taxes and administrative expenses can prove burdensome for many. Here again life insurance comes to the rescue of the man of wealth. For example, you can convert, at age 50, $33,000 of bonds or stocks into approximately $50,000 single premium (nonpar, O. L. used for illustration) fully paid-up contract, to increase greatly your estate costs fund. All you give up is the small current income on the $33,000 investments, and being in a high income tax bracket, this usually nets you only a small income anyway. Or, additional annual premium insurance will provide the increased estate tax costs fund at a nominal premium.

THE ECONOMIC VALUE OF A HOMEMAKER

Today's high taxes have produced an amazing upward spiral in the economic value of a full-time homemaker. Also, many women work outside the home and contribute substantially to their family income.

Typically, the full-time homemaker is a wife and mother. With every increase in the husband's income, a man's wife is worth more to him—as his estate grows, his wife's value becomes increasingly apparent. By the time a man reaches a position of wealth, his wife fairly dominates the financial picture.

Why is this? Because married couples have the privilege of filing a **joint income tax return,** thus saving many thousands of dollars during married life. Marriage also offers the advantage of the **marital deduction,** thus saving the estate a fortune in taxes when one spouse dies.

Conversely, when a man loses a non-working wife, he loses a tremendous financial asset in more ways than one.

No couple with a substantial income or estate can afford to overlook the value of a full-time homemaker when planning for the family's future security. "Spouse insurance" is the only practical solution.

ECONOMIC VALUE OF A HOMEMAKER

Services	*Hours Worked Per Week*	*Hourly Wage*	*Wages Per Week*
Dietitian	1.2	$17.10	$ 20.52
Launderer	5.9	14.85	87.62
Cook	13.1	14.00	183.40
Housekeeper	17.5	14.95	261.63
Nurses aide	44.8	8.00	358.40
Gardener	2.3	14.50	33.35
Secretary	2.0	14.45	28.90
Maintenance worker	1.7	15.00	25.50
Practical nurse	.6	15.02	9.01
Seamster	1.3	12.75	16.58
Dishwasher	6.2	7.85	48.67
Chauffeur	2.0	12.07	24.14
	98.6		$1,097.72

Annual Wage: $57,081.44*

*With children, add the services of a personal services specialist for an additional 168.0 hours per week at $16.60 per hour. This brings hours worked per week to 266.6 and adds $2,778.80 to wages per week, for a total weekly wage of $3,886.52 and an annual wage of $202,099.

Source: Michigan Department of Labor

AN IDEAL PROSPECT: THE YOUNG MAN OR WOMAN

You encounter these prospects everywhere: the young man or woman just out of school, employed, but as yet without family responsibilities. However, before you discuss the subject of life insurance with them, you must understand their point of view.

The young person is not concerned about death; he or she is full of life and vigor and having fun—and the thought of death is a foreign idea. The subject of retirement is of little interest, old age is so remote as to be almost unimaginable.

But there is an approach that's definitely appealing—the prospect of a **financial success.**

Base your sales story primarily upon the fact that the accumulation of capital is a tangible evidence of success—and that **life insurance is an essential part of a total financial plan.**

In most cases the young person will eventually be a married person with family responsibilities. Then he or she will need protection and lots of it. Try illustrating a whole life policy. Starting at these young ages, it's amazing how cash values build up in this type of contract.

QUOTES FOR YOUNG PEOPLE

With this plan your financial success is certain. **This is the one cash accumulation plan that is not based on "ifs."**

If you need money: this plan **guarantees it**—for business opportunities—for emergencies.
If you become sick or disabled: your cash values can continue to build, even though **you** can't go on working.
If you have to quit paying premiums: you'll still have a **substantial estate** that no one can take away.
If you die: your cash accumulation plan is **completed for you at once** and paid to anyone you choose.
If you grow old: you can never live long enough to spend the last dollar of lifetime income that's set aside for you.
THERE ARE JUST NO "IFS" ABOUT IT

" "

Many executives are asking of prospective young employees, "How much life insurance do you own?" And more and more application forms for important jobs ask for information about the amount of life insurance the applicant owns. **Think of the impression this life insurance plan will make!**

" "

The Law of Financial Success says: "Of all you earn, some is yours to keep and some is yours to spend." To make the law work, **first set aside what you determine to keep** and spend the rest. Otherwise, the law can never work for you.

" "

How would you like to start a life insurance plan which **will pay you about $6 in income for every $1 you set aside each month?** (Use your own company figures for the plan of your choice.)

" "

Would you like to be worth $100,000? Well, maybe you aren't now, but if you're the kind of young person your friends tell me you are, **you can be worth $100,000** before I leave.

MISCONCEPTIONS ABOUT THE YOUNG

They don't need life insurance, or don't need enough to make it worthwhile. FALSE. Just look at all of the needs they have:

1. **Funds for last expenses.**
2. **Proection of earning capacity** for the sake of dependents. Among young adults who live with their families, more than 90 percent contribute regularly to meet family expenses.

3. **A guaranteed accumulation or growth plan.** Young people are turning to investments that do not have the safety features of life insurance, because life insurance agents turn their backs on them.
4. **Retirement income.** This is especially true for women who try to quit work sooner and who will live, on the average, six years longer than men.
5. **Education for children.** They may help support their younger brothers, sisters, nieces and nephews. They often help support these children so that the youngsters may have some of the finer things in life.
6. **Mortgage cancellation.** (More homes now owned by younger adults.)
7. **Other.** (Business insurance, prevention of estate shrinkage and charitable bequests are more reasons why they may need life insurance.)

The young don't understand life insurance. FALSE. Let's be fair—how well does the average prospect understand insurance? How much explaining do you have to do? **Keep it simple.** Skip the technicalities. Sell the **benefits** and paint vivid word pictures.

Young people aren't practical. FALSE. Young people today are far more practical than they used to

> It's bad sales strategy to push your client into a corner—don't force a decision—your job is to help your prospect buy—*anon.*

be. They're usually better able to look the facts of life straight in the face.

TIPS ON SELLING TO THE YOUNG

Work by appointment. The average young working person is difficult to see during working hours. They may not have a private office and may feel uncomfortable spending time on personal affairs. It is better to make an appointment so they can arrange time to see you.

Don't use trick approaches. The young are suspicious of the slick salesperson. They resent being tricked and they don't like being high pressured. Tell them, frankly, that you are a life insurance agent and don't use a veiled approach. You may arouse curiosity for the moment, but the ultimate reaction may be unfavorable. Just be frank, courteous and pleasant.

Earn their confidence and respect. This ties in with the above. After the interview, the individual is going to talk about it to friends and family. If you earn respect and confidence right from the start, he or she will be talking **for** and not against you. Remember, this may be a potential center of influence.

Don't talk down to the young. Avoid such expressions as, "Do you follow me?," "Is that clear?", and the like. It is the **agent** who should be criticized if the prospect **doesn't** understand.

Don't underestimate young working people's buying power. Many young people are putting away considerable dollars a month. When you suggest that this accumulates only a few skimpy dollars a month, it's just another form of talking down.

Don't emphasize long premium paying periods. They may think that there's little chance of their working through to age 65. So policies with shorter payment periods are more attractive. If you do select a paidup at age 60 or 65 contract, show how he or she can stop payments earlier and either take their benefits or let them ride until later in life.

Soft-pedal the protection features. Unless the need for protection is vital, as in the case of dependent parents, make the death benefits an **extra**—a by-product of your plan.

Stress the safety of life insurance. Many individuals would rather not be continually worried about investment management. Emphasize the guarantees of the plan. The terms "loss proof" and "income for as long as you live" are likely to be favorably received.

QUOTES FOR THE YOUNG

Mr. or Ms. Prospect, this is an organized cash accumulation plan with **great flexibility. It** serves as **a retirement plan** to supplement and safeguard your Social Security benefit.

And we have these safety features: if you became sick or disabled so that you couldn't work anymore, my company will **make all of your payments for you** so that you will still have all the money you would have had. And you never have to pay back a penny! If you don't live to make many payments. **still** the plan **will be completed for you,** and all the money you would have had will be given at once to your beneficiary. Isn't that a wonderful plan!

" "

Don't say. "$10,000 maturity value." **Say,** "In 20 years the postman will bring you a check for $10,000." **Don't say,** "Whom do you want to be the primary beneficiary?" **Say.** "Whom do you want to receive all this money?" **Don't say.** "15-year cash value." **Say,** "In 15 years you can be lounging on a luxury liner with $5,000 in your purse." **Don't say,** "ten-year certain life income." **Say,** "It will be like finding an extra $25 under your breakfast plate every morning. Your only worry will be spending that $25 before another shows up."

CONSIDER THE FACTS

Over 62 million people in the U.S. are accident victims each year—about **170,000** every day—more than **7,000 every hour!**

The annual loss of income due to accidents is estimated at over $148 billion. Accidents **permanently** impair 380,000 people each year—**more than 1,000 each day!**

Over 3½ million workers a year suffer **prolonged illness** lasting, on the average, 14 days, one out of five illnesses will last over 90 days.

The cost of medical care has increased to record heights.

On an average day, five people out of every thousand are in hospitals. Annual hospital admissions are 16 per hundred.

These are not just cold facts. They represent people—people like you, and your friends and neighbors—many of whom were cut down by sickness or accident without warning. One day they were well and

SICKNESS AND ACCIDENT INCOME PROTECTION

On the average, THREE persons are dependent on the earnings of EACH employed individual. Think of the problem of providing for one's self, for dependents . . . of meeting the regular monthly bills . . . PLUS paying extra for medical care—ALL at a time when earned income has been cut off—when it is needed most!

On the following pages you will find indisputable facts, arresting ideas, dynamic phrases, a field-tested sales talk—to help you secure your share of the tremendous health and accident insurance market!

happy—working, paying bills, raising a family, buying a home. Then suddenly they are sick or disabled, economic liabilities to their families, instead of breadwinners.

It can happen to anyone, anytime—**and many people have inadequate sickness and accident protection—or no protection at all!**

REMEMBER THAT

One ordinary parent can support four children. But it takes four extraordinary children to support one parent.

> ALL INSURANCE IS GOOD IF YOU FIRST INSURE THE INCOME THAT PAYS THE PREMIUMS.

What do you think of the man who packs up and walks out on his wife and children? How much worse you would think of him if he stayed home and let his wife and children take care of him!

Someone carries the risk, always. Will it be you, your family or my company?

Each year you insure your home, yet chances of fire are one in 166. You insure your car, yet only one in 112 have an accident. You insure your life, of course, yet at age 35 your chances of dying are only one in 600. BUT THE CHANCES ARE ONE IN 15 THIS YEAR THAT YOU WILL BE DISABLED BY ACCIDENT ALONE. **What if disability lasts three months, six months, a year or more?**

Many people have good insurance programs—to protect their loved ones if death comes too soon. **But they have no income provision in case of prolonged disability!**

Such persons are financially better prepared to die than to live!

THE ABILITY TO EARN

The most valuable asset most people possess is their ability to earn money. I imagine this is true in your case, as it is in mine. Is that right?

Your income forms the foundation on which your family's living rests. It provides food three times a day, pays for a home, gives you and your family better-than-average clothes. It pays your insurance premiums, provides a car and some luxuries. After all that, there is probably a little left over for savings.

When this foundation—your income—is snatched from under your family, and you are unable to work due to sickness or accident, what happens? Your regular expenses continue, while extra expenses pile up. Your savings soon turn into a deficit. You go into debt deeper and deeper the longer you are disabled.

There are generally two stages to every sickness or accident. First, there is the critical stage where you need immediate treatment. Perhaps your doctor says you must go to the hospital. This is the

> By the way, have you arranged to have the life insurance company pay your premiums if you are seriously disabled?

shorter of the two phases. As soon as you start to recuperate you enter the second phase. This is the long period necessary to recover. You may have been in the hospital just a few days or a week—your doctor may tell you that you will have to be home for several months or half a year or even a year or longer. What will you do after your paycheck stops?

Wouldn't you like my company to pay you tax-free income while you are unable to work?

3

Prospecting Tips and Telephone Techniques

In the business of selling life insurance, a constantly flowing supply of prospects is vital to success. The prospecting tips on the following pages should help to create dozens of prospects each week.

The telephone is also an effective and time-saving working tool in making appointments. Included in the following pages are field-tested techniques of telephone usage.

A study of and the use of these working tools will bring you handsome rewards.

SOURCES OF PROSPECTS

Selling begins with finding a prospect. Since selling is an active process, so must prospecting be. It is seeking potential buyers of your product. It is uncovering raw material in which you can invest your personal capital of time and know-how.

Prospecting is not a separate job. It is a major link in the sales process. Just as you work at the job of selling each day, prospecting must become a daily habit to provide the constant supply of prospects that is so essential to success.

Where are prospects found? They come from two sources—from **within** and **without**. Your prospects are people **you know** and think about—and people **others know** and tell you about. In either case, unearthing prospects takes a bit of digging, and the digging tools you use are **questions.**

QUESTIONS TO ASK YOURSELF

1. *Whom do I know from my old job?*

Former employers, associates, employees . . . former customers or clients . . . former suppliers . . . former competitors.

2. *Whom do I know because I went to a certain school?*

Classmates . . . fraternity brothers . . . organization associates (athletic, dramatic, debating, etc.) . . . teachers . . . parents of classmates.

3. *Whom do I know because I enjoy a particular hobby or sport?*

Fellow enthusiasts of photography, chess, music, golf, tennis, bowling, home movies, travel, public speaking, dramatics . . . people who supply hobby or sports equipment.

4. *Whom do I know because of public service contacts or charitable interests?*

Church or temple contacts . . . community fund activities . . . other welfare work . . . YMCA associates.

5. *Whom do I know because I own my home?*

The real estate salesperson . . . former owner . . . builder . . . building supply personnel . . . various workers . . . landscapers.

6. *Whom do I know in my present or former neighborhood?*

Present neighbors and friends . . . former neighbors . . . store owners from whom I used to buy.

7. *Whom do I know because I drive a car?*

Dealer . . . salespeople . . . gas station owner . . . tire supplier . . . auto insurance agent . . . mechanics.

8. *Whom do I know because of what I buy?*

Grocer . . . pharmacist . . . owners and salespeople where I buy clothes . . . coal or oil dealer . . . dairy and laundry sales representatives . . . dry cleaner . . . hardware merchant . . . and all other people to whom I pay money for goods and services.

9. *Whom do I know because I have children?*

Their teachers . . . parents of their playmates . . . school principals . . . their special teachers, music, swimming, art, etc.

10. *Whom do I know because of my spouse's activities?*

Friends, associates, club members . . . civic projects . . . sports and recreation . . . PTA . . . alumnae association . . . church groups.

11. *Whom do I know from my own contacts?*

Associates . . . suppliers . . . clubs and organizations . . . car dealers, etc.

QUESTIONS TO ASK OTHERS

Standard Opening: Bill (or Mr. Center of Influence), I don't expect you to know anyone who wants to buy life insurance **today.** Even though I'm in the business, I don't know anyone like that either. My job, after meeting people, is to determine their need for life insurance, if any.

In asking FRIENDS for prospects: I don't want to impose on our friendship by asking favors for **myself.** Suppose I ask you to do a favor for five **other** friends of yours. Assume that any one of these friends of yours were to die, but prior to his death you had been given the opportunity of providing a lifetime income for his widow . . . or cancelling his mortgage . . . or guaranteeing that the children would be well educated . . . or making sure that they had plenty of food and clothing—and none of these things would cost you one cent. You'd certainly be glad that you had that opportunity wouldn't you? Well, actually you have that opportunity at this very moment. It could very well be that someone you know can use my services sooner than you think. I know you're not planning to go into the life insurance business, but if you were—**who are the first five people you would call on?**

In asking your own POLICYOWNERS: Maybe you'll recall, I was referred to you by a mutual friend. Even if we had never done business together, our meeting was a pleasant one. And I believe you are glad that you accepted my services. (Assume he says yes.)

Then you may have a friend who'd be interested in hearing about this service, too. I don't know his name, but I picture him as a man between 25 and 45, married, with at least one dependent child, having a steady job and good business judgment. **Whom do you know who fits that description?**

In asking BUSINESS PEOPLE: You will agree one of the marks of a successful business person today is an adequate and properly arranged life insurance program. I'm sure, too, that because of your position you have become acquainted with many young people who seem to have the mark of future success—real executive material. Those are the ones I'd like to know for I feel I can be of most help to them as they progress in the business world. **With that thought in mind, whom would you suggest I see first?**

In asking CLERGY: Just as you daily minister to people's spiritual needs, so it is my job to minister to them financially, that is, to help them solve their financial problems. And you are in an excellent position to help me help them. You know of births, engagements, marriages—all the good reasons for people to review their insurance programs. A little foresight on their part can prevent many of the financial tragedies which you have witnessed in the past. **With that**

thought in mind, whom would you suggest I see first?

In asking FARMERS: You farmers know all about the importance of insurance. When you fight against heat and cold, rain, frost, drought, pests and livestock diseases you are insuring. But very few people know enough about insuring their lives to prevent economic loss to their families—or about guaranteeing the comfort of an income, in old age. That's the kind of advice I'm in a position to give. **With that thought in mind, whom would you suggest I see first?**

A HANDY DATA GUIDE

Names alone are simply suspects. They may become **prospects** when you uncover helpful information about them. Memorize the phrase "NO RAIDS." It will guide you in obtaining at least seven important pieces of information.

N — name
O — occupation

R — residence
A — age
I — income
D — dependents
S — special interests

> There are few better feelings in the world than having lined up a week's worth of appointments before lunch on Monday—*anon.*

USING THE TELEPHONE TO SECURE APPOINTMENTS

Modern business accepts the telephone as a helpful servant. The life agent willing to study the use of the telephone can make it an invaluable assistant. There is one cardinal principle that must be accepted if the telephone is to be of genuine value to you. **You must have faith in the power of the telephone to help you do more effective work.**

Direct mail, cold canvass or any other plan of prospecting will be of little value if you have no faith in it. Do not try the telephone plan if you are unwilling to have faith in it. Do not use the telephone plan if you do not intend to give it a fair trial. Do not use it if you are unwilling to make a sincere effort to master the principles of telephone usage. If you undertake the work in a serious way, these suggestions will be helpful:

1. Put all the sincerity and enthusiasm possible into your voice. Make your voice say to the prospect that you are interesting and worth meeting.

2. Remember that your purpose in calling is to get an interview. Do not permit the prospect to draw you into an attempt to sell insurance over the phone unless the circumstances are most unusual.
3. Be courteous to the receptionist or secretary, but try to get connected with the prospect without telling your story to the receptionist or secretary.
4. An effective reply to the secretary or receptionist asking, "What do you wish to speak to Mr. (or Ms.) Prospect about?" is "Oh, I want to speak to him (or her) directly. Is he (or she) there?" Most secretaries are not accustomed to this use of the word "directly" and consequently will put the prospect on the phone at once.

   If the secretary insists on knowing your business, say in a courteous, firm manner, "I would be happy to tell you about the matter but it is personal and I am hesitant about discussing it with anyone other than Mr. (or Ms.) Prospect." This will almost invariably get you through.
5. If you are following up a referred lead, for example, simply tell the operator, "My name is Mr. Robert Underwood, and Mr. Davis of the XYZ Company suggested I get in touch with Ms. Prospect."

   If you are following up direct mail, tell the operator, "The matter is in regard to a letter I sent

> About the telephone "Say what you have to say, then get off"—*Ben Feldman*

Ms. Prospect last week, Monday. I think she will recall getting it."

6. In using the telephone for making appointments for first interviews, you will find most prospects' answers in these seven classes:
   a. in rare cases, you will get a "Yes," and then you have only to set the hour for the interview,
   b. the reply will be "No, I cannot see you,"
   c. "I have no money to put into more life insurance,"
   d. "Put your proposition in a letter,"
   e. "I'm not interested,"
   f. "I'm too busy to see you now" or
   g. "I have an agent who handles my insurance."

   In making appointments for first interviews, it is helpful to set up on small cards sound answers to each of the seven prospect objections. Keep those cards before you at the phone while calling. In this way you are always prepared to give the prospect a thoughtful, sensible answer. This plan will soon make you proficient in using the phone.
7. Keep in mind that constant use of the question, "Will it be more convenient to see you at 9:00 in

the morning or will 4:00 in the afternoon be better for you?" turns many a preliminary "No" into an appointment.

8. When necessary, bring into the first call arresting ideas as the Common Disaster Clause, the Spendthrift Clause, the Tax Savings idea, the Social Security Insurance Coordination idea and so on.
9. Do not overlook these valuable phone uses:
   a. birthday congratulations,
   b. age changes,
   c. to confirm appointments,
   d. to thank the prospect for seeing you and to create an opening for a later call,

WORKING CAPITAL

Many a business has gone bankrupt trying to operate on limited capital. Similarly, many a potential life underwriter has failed because of trying to operate on limited capital. OUR CAPITAL, OF COURSE, IS OUR PROSPECT FILE. It is our bank account. If we keep on making withdrawals and not making sufficient deposits WE GO BROKE—it is just that simple.—*J. H. Templin, CLU*

e. to use the approach, "I would like to see Mr. Policyowner about Policy No. 124356" with orphan leads and
f. to secure referred leads from present clients.

Look upon the telephone as one more valuable selling assistant. Use it as a time-saver in every way possible. Underwriters experienced in using the telephone are able to secure from six to eight appointments in one hour's use of the phone. Is any prospecting effort you now use bringing such results?

4

Power Phrases That Sell

Here are hundreds of words and phrases that are vibrant—motivating—alive with meaning.

These power phrases have opened up countless interviews in the past—are wrapping up many sales every day. They will help you immeasurably in your sales work, if you will take them and make them a part of your vocabulary.

That's why this chapter was written. We don't know who coined the invaluable phrases it contains. But we are glad somebody did, and we are glad we can share them with you.

IN THE APPROACH

- ••• Have you measured your present insurance against the job you want it to do?
  - *Do your insurance policies give you everything your premium entitles you to?*
- ••• Does your insurance go directly to your family or does it go through the courts?
  - *Are you sure that none of your children are disinherited?*
- ••• Are you being unfair to your younger children?
  - *Would you like to create a rich person's estate today?*
- ••• Do you know the pension power of your life insurance?
  - *Is your life insurance insured?*
- ••• Death comes everyday to someone and someday to everyone. I may be the last life insurance agent you will ever talk to.
  - *If you can save as much money in the next five years as you have in the last five years, will your will be satisfied?*
- ••• If you sold me the rights to all your future salary checks, what price would you set?

- *Have you taken steps to turn these rights over to your spouse in case of your premature death?*

••• Will Rogers said, "If a man doesn't believe in life insurance, let him die once without it. That will teach him a lesson!"

••• Have the proceeds of your policies been protected against your beneficiary's creditors?

- *Why did you buy the life insurance you now own?*

••• You may be able to say, "I don't need it," but can you say, "We don't need it"?

- *Have you any insured investments?*

IN THE INTERVIEW

••• Life insurance doesn't take money away from your family. It assures them money for future delivery—at the time they will need it most.

- *Some people spend their whole lives accumulating an estate no larger than the one I am offering you for a small deposit.*

••• A man of 35 has 30 years to save for himself, but he may have only 30 days to save for his family.

- *You pay a bank 9 percent or more for a debt. You pay us 3 percent for an asset.*

WHAT OTHERS SAY

"Life insurance is truly a basic institution in American Life. It offers real hope, real planning for the future, real saving and real protection for one's family."—*Margaret Chase Smith*

••• Do you know that each year you live reduces your spouse's chances of earning a living when you pass away?

••• Life insurance is the greatest expression of a person's love for family. It is the sincerest love letter ever written.

••• Yes, inflation is a constant threat. But is there anything that will inflate faster than a mother's financial problems upon her husband's death?

• *When you die, there will be three deaths: a husband, a father, and an income. The first two are irreplaceable—but I can help you with the third.*

••• You don't buy life insurance because you're going to die, but because they are going to live. And living takes money.

- *The wife should be left something that will take care of her—not something she will have to take care of.*

••• If you live, it is thrift. If you die, it is insurance.

- *The most valuable gift any father can leave his children is their mother's time and attention.*

••• There is nothing more uncertain than life and nothing more certain than life insurance.

- *In case of death. the bank pays what you have saved. But the life insurance company pays what you meant to save.*

••• The only thing a husband can buy on the installment plan for which his widow won't finish the payments after he dies, is life insurance.

- *The cost of a life insurance policy increases each year if you don't have it, and decreases if you do have it.*

••• When the family gets back from the funeral, the dollars from this policy will be waiting on the front porch.

- *After the doctor, nurse and undertaker get their share, there may be just about enough left to pay your spouse's bus fare down to work and back each day.*

- ••• With this plan, all of these benefits are our obligation. Without it, they become your obligation.
  - *No one knows how large the investment return will be, for no one knows how long you are going to live.*
- ••• The only person who takes a chance on life insurance is the one who does without it.
  - *Women with children have full-time jobs as mothers—they require an income to hold that job.*
- ••• You'd give your life for your children. Why not insure your life for them?
  - *If you had to go on a long trip for several months, how much money would your wife need each month you are gone? Would she need less if you were gone forever?*
- ••• Would you pay $1,000 for $1,000 of life insurance? That's what your widow would pay if you don't have it.
  - *The only thing worse than a home without a mother is a mother without a home.*
- ••• When there is a mortgage cancellation plan, it is the mortgage that walks out, not the family.

- *The family that needs a home while you are here will need it twice as badly if you are not here.*

••• If you buy this policy, you can say to your child, "When I am 65, you'll probably hear me knocking at your door. But don't get worried. It will be for a weekend, not a lifetime."

- *Life insurance will come to you when you are 65 and say, "Relax, from now on I'll pay the bills."*

••• If someone were to agree to mail your family a $1 bill each month after you die, would you be willing to pay about a portion of the postage on it in advance?

- *The difference between an old person and an elderly lady or gentleman can be income.*

••• The misery of old people, alone and without income, is of interest to nobody but themselves.

- *True wealth is money to spend, not money to manage.*

••• Old age can last a long time, but not one day longer than the life income option of insurance.

- *Life insurance makes your money work for you when you are through working for it.*

••• No one plans to be poor in old age. But many just don't make plans not to be.

- *It would be like coming down to breakfast every morning after age 65 and finding a brand-new $20 bill under your plate.*

••• Unless you have rich relatives, the only money you will have at retirement age is the money you don't spend now.

- *The heaviest burden an old person can carry is an empty wallet or purse.*

••• How would you like 52 weeks' vacation with pay?

- *Old age needs so little, but it needs that little so much.*

••• When a man reaches 65, he is either glad he did buy life-insurance or sorry that he didn't.

- *There are two ways of getting the necessities of life in old age—with money or with self-respect.*

- *You ask, "How much life insurance do I need?" Nobody can tell you. Suppose you ask yourself, "How much do I love my wife and children?" There's your answer.*

- *Don't leave your home to chance—leave it to your family.*

••• Death creates the need for immediate cash—life insurance creates immediate cash for the need.

- *Your child may have a "right" to a good education. but it's going to take money to exercise that "right."*

IN CLOSING

••• Do you ever want your children embarrassed by anything you didn't do that you could have done?

- *Do you know how long you are going to stay in good health?*

••• Within a few months, every company in America is going to raise your rate.

- *Whatever reason you may have for not starting this plan now will only sound ridiculous to your widow.*

••• I know you believe in getting experienced advice before you make decisions. Why not ask someone who can't get life insurance if you should wait awhile?

- *Life insurance is always paid for, whether a man buys it or not. It's just a question of who pays, the man—or his widow—or the old man he will be.*

> **WHAT OTHERS SAY**
>
> "... Even a poor man can build up an estate with life insurance. When he does create such an estate, he can feel real satisfaction in knowing that his family is protected if anything happens."—*President Harry Truman*

••• You had this financial problem before I came to see you; you've got it now, and you'll continue to have it after I'm gone—unless you do something about it now. Postponing the solution doesn't postpone the problem.

• *Your wife may have to train herself to get her old job back. Do you have an educational policy for your wife?*

••• If you start this plan now and decide to quit a year later, you'd lose $200, which wouldn't be too serious. However, if you don't start it and you die within a year, your family would lose $10,000. Wouldn't it be easier for you to overcome a $200 loss than for your family to overcome a $10,000 loss?

• *Your beneficiary will not be your wife, but your widow. And widows never object to life insurance.*

- *Which will be easier—for you to give up a few luxuries now, or for them to give up many necessities later?*

••• Can you think of any future contingency which will make you regret having purchased this insurance? Can you think of any contingency which will make you very glad that you did purchase it?

••• Life insurance isn't an added obligation—it's your best means for meeting the obligations you already have.

- *If you and your family have a tough time now getting by on your salary, how can they possibly get by without it?*

••• More good things are lost by indecision than by wrong decision.

- *You have told me you wanted to solve these financial problems for your family and yourself. In case you do not go ahead with this plan, what plan are you going to use? Or are you just going to let the problem go unsolved?*

••• Could you certify that the answers to these questions are correct?

- *Just sign this request to obligate the company, and we'll make arrangements to see the doctor.*

••• So that we may submit a personalized plan for you, would you please answer the following questions?

- *How would your wife like to have her name appear on these checks?*

••• Would you prefer to have the premium notices sent to your home or your office?

- *Do you have any reason to believe that you cannot pass the physical examination?*

••• If you die tonight, will your relatives give your widow the amount of money promised by this plan? Will your employer? Will anyone? Then don't you want the life insurance company to do it?

- *Life is not a waiting proposition—nor is life insurance.*

••• The man who fails to protect his mortgage is betting with his family that he will live long enough to pay it off. Can your family afford stakes that high?

••• You wouldn't send your spouse a present in a C.O.D. package, would you? (In closing a mortgage cancellation presentation.)

- *There are two kinds of widows: widows with homes and homeless widows. Which will your wife be?*

••• If you're worried about the cost, think about the cost of having too little,

••• Yesterday is gone . . . tomorrow never comes . . . that leaves only today to start this plan

- *The misery of a child is interesting to its mother; the misery of a young man is interesting to a young woman: but the misery of an old man or old woman is interesting to nobody.*

HOW PROMINENT PEOPLE HAVE FELT ABOUT LIFE INSURANCE

President John F. Kennedy: ". . . I know of no better investment for the future of a family than life insurance. I know of no American enterprise that better symbolizes individual initiative and financial independence than the life insurance companies of America."

President Dwight D. Eisenhower: "One of the clearest evidences of the faith of our people in the free institutions and the future of America is the fact that 90 million of our citizens own life insurance policies.

Their ownership of life insurance is more than a 304 billion dollar bulwark of family protection. It also is a kind of thrift which provides productive capital. This capital, invested in farms, factories, homes, transportation, utilities and other resources, helps to give this nation the economic power needed to buttress freedom in the world."

Polly Bergen: "Ask any mother why life insurance is very important and she'll probably point to her children as the answer. Her family is her most important possession. The finest act she can perform for her children is to make their futures as secure as possible. Through life insurance, the family is prepared for any occurrence. It gives children the best security. Nest eggs have a way of dwindling; the family bank account is taken for immediate projects. Insurance planning is not only the answer, but it is the best solution for her."

Bob Hope: ". . . I've seen many actors, many of whom bunked in the star's dressing room with that gold star on the door, pass on with little left for their dependents. First things first—and one of the first things on anyone's mind should be adequate life insurance. You don't have to be an actor to know that life insurance plays an important role in your own story."

George Gallup, famous for public opinion research work: "What worldly goods does the young bridegroom need today? **Life insurance** was named first by persons in all age groups, by those with the most education, by professional and business people, and by white collar families."

Philip B. Gilliam, Juvenile Court Judge: "Each day I face a parade of young people gone wrong. There are many reasons why they appear in my court, but one underlying cause keeps cropping up.

"These boys and girls have lost their feeling of security, the sense of being loved. And with it has gone the incentive to love and respect others.

"Young people need a lot of parental love in their lives. That means supplying the sturdy discipline they require and unknowingly crave. And it means giving wisely of yourself, your experience and judgment.

"The buying of life insurance, it always seems to me, is an outstanding example of love at work to achieve added soundness and unity within the family. In addition to its long-range protection, it lends fresh strength for confident and happy living. It often goes far to create a background of family stability that keeps a child on the right track."

5

Handling Objections

Real objections merit sound answers, for when they are removed, the sale is usually made.

Skilled underwriters know that objections are either real or simply excuses. If they are plainly excuses. the best plan is to continue with your interview.

This section gives you strong answers to objections, each stressing a different point, so you will be able to give the prospect a sound answer to valid objections and be armed for virtually any objection that may arise.

> Never, ever accept a no from anyone—especially from yourself—*Sidney Friedman*

TYPES OF OBJECTIONS

Classifying objections is helpful in preparing to meet them in the field. Most objections fall into these major groups:

1. **No Need:** Prospects who use this objection are not opposed to life insurance, but they believe they have provided enough security for themselves and their families.
2. **No Time:** Prospects are too busy to talk to you. This may mean they don't want to be disturbed, mentally; don't want to think about the consequences of being underinsured.
3. **No Interest:** Prospects are covering up the real objection. Their reason for not wanting to discuss life insurance may be any of the objections listed.
4. **No Money:** Prospects may realize they need more life insurance, but feel financially unable to buy it—or feel a more pressing need to put their money into current purchases—a new car, a TV, freezer, etc.

5. **No Confidence:** Prospects prefer other investments to life insurance, or prefer another agent or another company.
6. **No Hurry:** Prospects fear to make a decision and want to put it off.

Although there may be some overlapping, this grouping will serve as a useful approach to the study of objections.

HAVE ALL I WANT (OR NEED)

That's a perfectly honest statement, and I'll be equally honest. Since you have no intention of buying more life insurance—and since I make my living selling insurance—then everything I say from this point on must be to **your** advantage and not to **mine.**

" "

In that case, congratulations! By the way, does each policy carry a common disaster clause? Spendthrift clause? Automatic premium loan? And are you familiar with the pension power of your life insurance?

" "

Perhaps you don't need more insurance, but can you include your family in that statement and say, "We don't need more"? Life insurance is a **family matter.** Think of it in terms of WE, and then of your wife as a widow trying to maintain the home, educate the children, and retain a decent standard of living. Could she do it on the income from your present insurance?

" "

Fine, Ms. Prospect. You have all the life insurance you need from the standpoint of the family. But how about **yourself?** Have you arranged a big enough paycheck for **yourself** when you can no longer work? And until then, could you use extra capital, in cold cash, for some business opportunity, or in case some emergency should arise?

HAVE ENOUGH INSURANCE

Then you are very fortunate. Not one person in ten has enough. Perhaps you had sufficient insurance when you bought last, but is it true today, considering your family's higher standard of living, rising costs, and changes in your family situation? Or is it possible

> If you had bought more insurance ten years ago, would you be better off today? That being the case, isn't today the time to prevent regrets ten years from now?

that you have **too much** insurance. May I suggest that we find out definitely?

INSURANCE POOR

I used to feel the same way until I compared what my life insurance would do for my family if I should die with what my earnings would do for them if I stay alive. You're earning about $30,000 a year and there's about 30 years until retirement. That means a total future income of at least $900,000. You say you have $90,000 insurance. So if you die, **you'd be worth about ten cents on the dollar.** It does look like your **family** would be "insurance poor."

" "

Most people who think they are "insurance poor" are really "insurance rich." They don't realize **what wonderful property they own,** or how large a part of their premium dollar is going into cash accumulation. That's what I want to talk about—the life insurance you now own.

" "

I'm glad to hear that. How have you arranged your insurance to give your family the most security? ("How" is a magic word for getting a prospect to talk and think seriously about his or her situation.)

I'VE HAD MY INSURANCE PROGRAMMED

I congratulate you! However, in recent years certain tax laws (or Social Security amendments) have been exacted that have a direct bearing on everybody's life insurance program. **Has your program been reviewed this year?**

" "

That shows good thinking on your part. However, life insurance programs have a way of becoming obsolete quickly in our changing economy. I have examined many programs that were excellent at one time but have become **hopelessly out of date.** If your program is still in good shape, I'll be the first to tell you. Then you will have the benefit of a double check.

" "

It's good to know that you have not neglected this important matter. Would you mind telling me how you have arranged to deal with the children **equally,** considering their different ages? Is the whole program insured against a prolonged sickness or a serious accident? (Or other questions that the prospect may not be able to answer readily, thus arousing the prospect's curiosity and giving you an opening.)

" "

Fine, Mr. or Ms. Prospect, now in working it out, did you take into consideration the **tremendous**

PESTERED BY AGENTS

How wrong, how tragically wrong, is the point of view: "I wish life insurance agents wouldn't pester me all of the time!"

Thank God that they are pestering you. The day the most life insurance agents call on you should be one of your happiest days.

For it means you are in good health; otherwise they would not call. It means you are financially solvent, thrifty of mind and purpose. It means you are sound morally. It means people believe you are a good citizen, anxious to play the game with your family. OTHERWISE LIFE INSURANCE AGENTS WOULD NOT CALL.

The saddest day in your life will be the day the life insurance agents of your community give you the cold shoulder, when they never knock at your door!

For if that day comes, it will mean that you are going to pieces physically. Or going to pieces morally. Or going to pieces financially.

Be glad for every agent who calls on you—and make sure you do something about the problems they discuss, before they stop forever calling on you.—*Paul Speicher*

monetary value of your spouse? Have you analyzed the dollar losses that would result from his or her death, and the tragic effect these losses will have on the future financial security of the family? (See page 68.)

I'M TOO BUSY

Mr. (or Ms.) Prospect, I intend to be brief and to the point. In fact, **it will take just five minutes for you to decide if what I have to offer is of real value to you.** Just look at your watch. After five minutes, simply point at it and I'll end the discussion—unless you want me to go on. That's fair enough, isn't it?

" "

The reason you are so busy is that you are working eight hours a day, or more, to provide enough dollars for you and your family. Right? **Then wouldn't it be wise to take just ten minutes to protect the income for which you work so hard?** I'm busy, too, but I'll be glad to give that much time to be of help to you.

" "

I realize there are occasions when a person can't take time out just at the moment. I'm sure you **really are** busy and I will not impose on you now. I will leave it to you to tell me when you'll have a few free minutes. Perhaps Friday at 10 A.M. would be convenient, or would 4 P.M. be better?

" "

Of course you are; I expected that you'd be busy. But if I told you I had a $10,000 check for you or Mrs. Prospect, would you be able to spare a few minutes to talk to me about it? Well, **I could** be the man who might deliver such a check.

I DON'T CARE TO DISCUSS IT

You don't want to discuss life insurance? All right, let's talk about **time** insurance!

What would it be worth to you to know, without any doubt, that you'd live long enough to pay off the mortgage on your home, educate the children, finish saving enough money so the family would never have to worry about finances?

What would it be worth to you to have a guarantee that all these things would be done?

" "

That's a frank statement and exactly what most people say before they have a brief outline of our plan. **May I have just five minutes to give you the high points?**

" "

Would you be interested if I can show you a way to obtain from 15 percent to 25 percent additional benefits from your present life insurance—without any additional cost to you?

" "

I understand what you mean when you say you won't discuss it, Mr. Prospect. **You mean that you're not interested in spending any more money right now,** and I don't blame you. It's hard enough to get ahead these days, and that's what I came to talk about—an easier way to get ahead and have some of your hard-earned dollars for yourself.

I CAN'T AFFORD IT

When we say we "can't afford" something, aren't we usually speaking of luxuries? But life insurance is no luxury. It is **food, clothing, shelter, education and other things that are absolutely necessary for your family.**

" "

Let's look at it from another point of view. **Can your family afford to be without this plan?** Can your wife afford to be a widow? Can your children afford to be without income to provide what they need? This plan means a sacrifice for you of a few dollars a week. **In comparison with the sacrifices your family would have to make without it, what do a few dollars amount to?**

" "

You say you can't afford this plan. Then, I can say very seriously that I think you need this plan more than ever. If your income were cut 10 percent, you

could readjust, couldn't you? **But with the family bills still coming in, how could your family manage a 75 percent or 85 percent cut in income?**

I guess I haven't done a very good job explaining this plan. It means food on the table and clothes on the backs of your children and heat in your home. When you think of these necessities, **the word "afford" seems out of place, doesn't it?** Isn't it a matter of rearranging your budget so that if you die your family can afford to go on living—and **want** to go on?

" "

Can you put aside $1 a month? (Yes.) Can you put aside $1,000 a month? (No.) **Then there must be some amount between $1 and $1,000 that you can manage to put aside.** Can you put aside $350 a month? $250? (Keep suggesting amounts until you peg the amount he agrees he can put aside. Then write the application for that size policy.)

AFRAID I CAN'T KEEP IT UP

If you knew that you'd be called on to pay only one premium, you'd scrape it up somehow, wouldn't you? **It could be** that the one premium is all you'd ever have to pay. You don't know. I don't know. Isn't it safer to assume that it may be the **only** premium than not to buy because you are afraid that you couldn't pay the **next** premium?

" "

Tell me, Mr. Prospect, when were you married? (Five years ago.) And when you said "I do," were you **sure** you could help provide for your wife the rest of your life? Were you **sure** you could buy a home and keep it well furnished? And when little Joan was born, as you looked at her through that window in the hospital, were you **sure** you could give her everything she would need in life? Or, at these times, **did you just stick out your chin a little and resolve to do your level best?** Do Mrs. Prospect and Joan deserve any less now—any less than your level best to see that they're always provided for?

" "

Do you drive to work? (Yes.) **Do you wait in front of your house until the lights are green all the way to town?** Or do you start out and take the lights and other driving conditions as they come? I'm sure you start out, confident in your ability to get yourself where you want to go.

" "

The answer to that is built right into the plan. Suppose you continue the premiums for only five years and then find you're financially embarrassed. We'll guarantee you a paid-up estate of. . . . (Explain the nonforfeiture provisions, also the automatic premium loan clause which takes care of a **temporary** lack of funds.)

CAN'T HANDLE ANY MORE OBLIGATIONS RIGHT NOW

I understand how you feel, but I'm not suggesting that you add to your obligations. **This is an opportunity to discharge some of the obligations you already have**—those you undertook when you were married and started raising a family. By owning this insurance, you actually will have **fewer** obligations, not more. **You'll be transferring the heaviest obligations to the shoulders of my company**—obligations of a permanent family home—income to live on—educations for the children. Also the obligation to the old person you'll be someday—if you live.

" "

Most people I talk to don't consider the purchase of life insurance as taking on an obligation—any more than the purchase of food. Life insurance is an essential. It is food, clothing and shelter—and adequate insurance should be built right in the family budget. Otherwise, you are sidestepping your most serious obligations.

" "

It's not unusual that you have current obligations—unpaid bills, installment purchases, and the like. But, Mr. Prospect, wouldn't they still have to be paid if you die? And isn't your wife the one who'd have to pay them? Why not make sure that after paying off your obligations she'd have enough to live on?

GOING TO BUY A CAR

And when you buy your car, you won't even start the motor until you arrange car insurance **to protect the widow of the man you might accidentally kill while driving that automobile.** Shouldn't you first protect your spouse who, if **you are the victim of an accident, will become your widow?**

SAVING TO BUY A TELEVISION (CAR, REFRIGERATOR, ETC.)

I'm all for that, Ms. Prospect. You should have those nice things, and that is what this plan is for. You're a person who is considerate of her family's welfare, and just think of the money you'd have to set aside to give them some measure of security—**if there were no such thing as life insurance.** To leave them only a year's income, you would have to save $3,000 a year for ten years—or $6,000 a year for five years. **How much of your income would be left to buy a TV (car, etc.)?** But a payment of only $______ creates the $30,000 for your family at once and leaves you free to spend all the rest of your income as you please.

> You don't have to buy a newspaper to find out how much your life insurance is worth.

WE'RE PLANNING TO BUY A HOUSE

Then it's a matter of making a **balanced decision.** You don't want so much insurance that you can't have the home, and you don't want to arrange such a big home payment that you can't have the insurance you need. A home is important. Adequate insurance is important. **Why not make a fair division of your income so you can have both?** If you get the insurance into your budget before you buy the house, you can extend the house payments a little longer and have both, a home and protection.

OUR BUDGET WON'T ALLOW IT

Budgeting is the only sensible way to handle money. And, **there are three kinds of budgets:** the family's budget today, the widow's budget, and the old-age budget. Today's family budget is the only one that is supported by your earning ability. In turn, today's budget must support the other two—**or there simply won't be anything for a widow or elderly man to budget.**

FRIEND IN THE BUSINESS

Does that mean regardless of how interesting a plan I, or any other insurance agent, were to show you, you would buy only from your friend? Are you obligated to buy all the rest of your life insurance from your friend?

" "

Mr. (or Ms.) Prospect, I've learned that many of my friends are using me as an excuse for putting off other insurance agents. Yet, I hesitated to press them to buy life insurance merely because I was their friend. I suspect your friend may have the same reluctance. Since I'm here I'd appreciate the opportunity of talking to you for a few minutes.

" "

I appreciate your telling me that, but so often I hear people say they don't want to handle business on a friendship basis. They prefer to have the services of an impersonal adviser and keep it on a **business basis.**

" "

Each of us must be pushed to do things we tend to put off, and our friends don't like to force us to take the action we know we should. Perhaps your friend has hesitated to inquire about such a personal matter as your basic financial obligations. Yet these obligations are the very reason you need adequate life insurance. You can rest assured that our relationship would be objective and confidential.

Someday you may want to use your cash value to make a business deal or to take care of some personal matter. When you need cash quickly, **do you want your close friends to know all about it?**

PREFER INVESTMENTS

For some purposes, other investments are just fine, but suppose we draw a parallel here. Did you let your family go without a home while you bought a board here and there . . . a sack of cement now and then . . . a few nails and bricks as you could afford them — hoping you would finally have enough materials to build a house? No—**you provide the home now,** when your family needs it. And you pay for it little by little.

Then should you let your family go without enough insurance while you save a bit here and there . . . buy a few stocks now and then . . . or mutual funds and bonds as you can . . . hoping you'll finally build an estate—**if you're lucky—if you have time?** Isn't it sensible **to provide the estate now, for your family may need it tomorrow.** And you can have the estate now and **pay for it later—ONLY THROUGH LIFE INSURANCE!**

" "

That's interesting. WHY do you prefer investments? (Let your prospects talk and they, themselves, will uncover their basic financial needs. Then you can explain how life insurance plus an investment program will best meet those needs.)

If you have to see a person on the 20th floor of a building, **do you walk up the stairs? No, you take an elevator** and you're up there in a moment or two.

Life insurance is the **elevator way** of building an estate. **As soon as the policy is in force, you have reached the heights of a substantial estate, so far as your family is concerned.** But when you save little by little and secure other investments as you can afford them, you are building up your estate one step at a time. If you slip and fall on one of the lower steps, **that's as far as your estate will go.** It might be wiser to take the elevator first and then concentrate on investments.

GOING TO BUY MUTUAL FUNDS

There's much to be said about mutual funds. Yet most investment advisers, including bankers and mutual funds executives, recommend **adequate permanent life insurance before money is put into any other investment.** My purpose is to help you determine whether your present insurance will provide a livable income for your family and a **guaranteed** amount of cash for you at retirement. Tell me, if you are removed from the family circle tomorrow, how much will they have to live on each month from now on?

" "

What is it that you really want to accomplish? Isn't it guaranteed security for your family and yourself? If that is true, then remember this: mutual funds have one possible advantage—the **chance** for a little more gain in value over the years. Life insurance, in comparison, offers **reasonable gain on a guaranteed basis PLUS tax advantages PLUS lifetime income from accumulated funds PLUS a tremendous gain for your family if you should die.** Actually, **there is no comparison—for there is no substitute for life insurance!**

" "

NOTE: We recommend that you avoid lengthy and heated discussions about the relative merits of mutual funds and life insurance. Concentrate on your prospect's financial objectives and strongly suggest that he or she take care of first things first. Security comes first . . . **and guaranteed security comes only from life insurance.**

I'M WORRIED ABOUT INFLATION

I'd be interested in your views on inflation. **Would you tell me what really worries you about it?** (This is intended to uncover the prospect's motive in bringing up inflation. Is it a bona fide objection or just a stall? If in earnest, the prospect should be led to understand that inflation calls for **more** insurance, not less.)

" "

It seems to me, Mr. (or Ms.) Prospect, that your principal concern should be **deflation,** not inflation. Just try to visualize the problems your family would face trying to live on the amount of life insurance you now own. **For them, that would be real deflation.**

We must remember **that life insurance is the only accumulation** (outside of cash savings and government bonds) **that will deliver a guaranteed number of dollars.** Everything else you own can fluctuate in value, including your house which is probably your largest single investment. Wouldn't it be wise to put **a sound base of fixed dollars — of known amount—** under your investment? Isn't this a good reason for life insurance?

" "

Don't you agree that a widow is more concerned about the definite **number** of dollars she'll get each month, rather than the inflated or deflated value of the dollar? If she knows exactly how much money she can count on, she can make out a budget with confidence.

I WANT TO THINK IT OVER

Very good, Ms. Prospect. **Let's think it over together.** Let me summarize some of the important points. For a $___ a month payment by you, my company will guarantee. . . . (Reemphasize the advantages of the plan.) I think that's a wonderful plan, don't you? How would Ms. Prospect like to have her name appear on her checks?

" "

That's all right. **But while you're thinking it over, my company has to do some thinking too.** We can't count, definitely, on your getting this plan. Let's make sure you have something **concrete** to think about by arranging a medical examination for you this afternoon.

" "

Isn't it true that a large factor in a person's progress is the **ability to make decisions?** You agree this plan is a good one; you say you can save this amount of money—why don't we make the right decision here and now, and put the plan in force?

" "

Naturally, a decision of this kind deserves some serious consideration. But thinking about it will not erase the **immediate** need for your family's protection. If you're taken away from the family before you have the privilege of reaching a decision, think how they would suffer. **Hasn't your family already made your decision for you?**

SEE ME LATER

All right, if you want to wait awhile that's certainly your privilege. But would you mind telling me what you're really waiting for? Are you waiting for good health? It looks to me like you're okay physically. **Are you waiting until you have a need?** We've already agreed the need will not be any less than it is now. **Are you waiting for money?** You appear to be a person who **could** put this program in force. **Are you waiting until you are a year older?** In that case your payments would be greater and you would get less out of it. Tell me honestly, what **are** you waiting for?

" "

You say to see you in a few months. But if you don't need the plan **now** why will you need **it then?** I don't want to sell you anything you don't need. But if you'll need it **then,** you need it every bit as much **now**—and every day you wait you are gambling with your family's future.

You say you are waiting for a raise after the first of the year. If you don't get it, **will you have to move—**

make your family do without new clothes—cut down on food? Of course not, but if you're taken away from the family before next year, **it is very likely that they will have to do all those things.**

WANT TO TALK IT OVER WITH MY SPOUSE

This is a business transaction, Mr. or Ms. Prospect. You and your spouse should make a joint decision.

" "

That's a good idea. It would be a better idea if we talked it over together with your wife. She is certain to have some questions which I might need to answer. In anything as important as this, she should have a clear understanding of the benefits for her, for you and for the family.

" "

Ms. Prospect, I have found that when it comes to life insurance, there are **three kinds of spouses. First** is the one who doesn't even want to think about the possibility of his or her dying. **Second** is the spouse who sees life insurance as a competitor for a new luxury. **Third** is the one who says to his or her spouse, "It's up to you." **But deep down inside they all say, "I'm glad he or she loves me enough to be so concerned about our future."**

" "

> Those who stand around saying it can't be done are usually interrupted by those who are doing it—*anon.*

That shows you are considerate of his wishes. But in this case you are really considering his future welfare, which he doesn't like to think about so long as you are there. If he said you should not take this plan and then you were taken from the family circle, **he would probably regret all the financial hardship and denial he caused the children.**

" "

Ms. Prospect, you may want to find out first if the company will accept you before you propose the idea to your husband.

" "

So long as you are here, Ms. Prospect, don't you feel that this is your responsibility? Your husband will have enough responsibility on his shoulders if you're not here.

6

Investments

In comparing life insurance to various investments, it is essential to understand the different types of investments that may be owned by the clients you serve. Also, this knowledge is invaluable in estate planning work.

INVESTMENTS

The selling and promotion of equity products was at one time not within the province of the life insurance agent. However, within the past few decades there has been more emphasis on total financial planning for the consumer, and now most life insurance salespersons are also marketing equity products. Today many life insurance companies require that their agents have a securities license as well as one for insurance.

The public needs to be educated about the field of equities. The great majority of consumers still prefer to save with guaranteed products. Indications from pension and profit-sharing plans that offer various investment options, including both guaranteed vehicles and securities, show that more than 75 percent of all employees have none of their funds in stocks. Only a little under 4 percent have 50 percent or more invested in the market. Many financial planners point out the danger of having too large a proportion of savings in fixed investments, because inflation substantially cuts into the value of fixed dollars.

As an example, someone saving $5,000 a year in a 6 percent fixed income account from age 40 to age 65 will accumulate $274,323 upon retiring. With even a conservative estimate of 4 percent annual inflation, the amount will be equal to $102,903 in 25 years. Adding to that the tax that must be paid on the deferral(s), the investor may fall behind.

However, averaging a 10 percent return over that same period of time (not an unusual result for quality equity investments), the same individual will accumulate $491,735, almost 80 percent more! This result should more than make up for income taxes and inflation.

Financial planners generally advise younger people to channel a large portion of their savings into common stocks to achieve substantial growth. As the investor gets older, a more conservative stance should be taken, although some portion of the portfolio should remain in equities after retirement, to counterbalance inflation.

The first objective of every investor should be security for self and dependents, which requires nonrisk assets that life insurance is uniquely qualified to supply. However, changing economic conditions may bring to the surface some of the calculated risks inherent in equity investments. A proper balance is the course that is needed, and the knowledgeable life insurance purveyor and equity advisor should be able to provide the counseling service needed.

MUTUAL FUNDS

One of the most popular investment products sold by dual-licensed insurance professionals is mutual funds. Consumers who might shy away from investing in stocks will be good prospects for mutual funds. The main reason for this is that these funds offer the opportunity for the relatively new investor to enter the stock market without being subject to many of the risks and costs involved in buying individual securities.

The managers of a mutual fund use the individual shareholders' contributions to purchase and manage a combined portfolio of many stocks, bonds and other investments. Individual securities are bought and sold (traded) as often as daily.

Mutual funds differ from each other according to their investment objectives. These objectives match consumer demands. Some investors desire a steady flow of income; this group of investors is most likely to be retirees not as interested in growth as they are in stability. Other investors will forego current income and would rather have as their goal long-term growth. There are also funds for short-term investors as well as for those seeking income tax advantages. There are balanced funds, providing both growth and current income, government securities funds, mortgage backed securities such as Ginnie Maes. The variety seems to be almost endless. Whatever the makeup, mutual funds will remain an important part of the American investment industry.

PROFESSIONAL ATTITUDE

There is ample proof that common stocks, investment real estate, many types of bonds, mutual fund shares, etc., cannot take the place of life insurance! Yet, these investment media are **essential** to the industrial growth and economic stability of the nation, for

> It is the responsibility of professional life underwriters to help individuals set up an ample reserve fund and a fully adequate insurance program.
>
> By the same token, the financial planner will not seek to encourage an individual to bank solely on guaranteed life insurance cash values or savings accounts in accumulating long-term monetary security. Inflationary pressures on the purchasing power of the dollar through the years must be considered. While there is some element of fluctuation in value with equity products, it is up to the counselor to help determine what proportion of risk is individually acceptable for each individual.

they help to channel idle funds into job-producing business activities.

Life insurance is also essential to the financial stability of the individual and the country's economic health. Thus, there is a responsibility placed on **both** the investment adviser and the life underwriter.

Suppose you could add these features to $10,000, $25,000 or more of stocks, bonds, real estate holdings, mutual fund shares, etc.

1. A Judgment Proof Clause.

> The most expensive possession you can have is a closed mind. It will cost you money all your life long—*anon.*

2. A Clause to Eliminate Probate Costs, Legal Fees and Delays in passing the property to your heirs.
3. A Depression Proof Clause—to guarantee your investment will never drop in price.
4. A Lifetime Income Clause—for you and for your spouse, too.
5. A Guaranteed Distribution Clause—at no added cost.
6. A Guaranteed Borrowing Power Clause—borrow 100 cents on your dollar values.
7. A Tax-Free Accumulation Clause—no current tax on value increases.
8. A Double Payout Clause if death is accidental.
9. An Automatic Self-Completion Clause if you become totally and permanently disabled—with all values continuing to build up.

THIS IS LIFE INSURANCE!

7

Total Needs Selling

This chapter is not an instruction in programming methods. Instead, the suggestions in these pages can be applied to any system of total needs selling you are now studying or using in the field.

Here are time-tested programming helps—gleaned from the experiences of outstandingly successful agents—ideas for use in the Approach, in Fact-Finding, in the Solution and in the Close. They will help you make your total needs selling interviews more effective.

GENERAL HINTS ON TOTAL NEEDS SELLING

What is programming? There is no standard definition of the term "programming." Some contend, and perhaps rightly so, that programming is simply the sale of a policy in proper relation to an applicant's overall needs and his or her other life insurance. In this light, the boundary line between single-need selling and program selling is indistinct.

Other agents think of programming as a mechanical or mathematical process. This involves a consideration of all the needs for cash and income that arise at the time a prospect dies, grows old or (in some cases) becomes disabled. The procedure also demands a study of the cash and income-producing potential of a prospect's estate, with special emphasis on the use of life insurance settlement options. The object, of course, is to reveal gaps in the prospect's program and to fill them with new life insurance.

But in its all-inclusive sense, the term "programming" covers much more ground: It begins with your approach to a prospect on the basis of a programming service—and it **never ends** as long as you have an unfilled service obligation to your client and the policyowner family.

APPROACH

- Securing the prospect's interest
- Gaining the prospect's confidence

FACT-FINDING

- Uncovering the prospect's needs
- Listing the prospect's resources
- Determining the deficiency
- Getting a commitment

SOLUTION

- Preparing the solution
- Presenting the proposal

CLOSE

- Getting the application
- Completing all service promised

Steps in a complete programming service. There are four steps in the programming process:

Approach, Fact-Finding, Solution and Close. The elements are present in either the one-interview or two-interview programming presentation.

No attempt will be made here to offer instruction on all these programming steps. Such an effort would be impractical in this brief section. Volumes have been written on the psychology and technique of the programming interview. Most agents have access to courses that give detailed instructions on the proper use of settlement options, on the mathematical procedures, on the use of charts or graphs, etc. Thus, the preparation for complete programming is a matter of intensive individual study or group training, coupled with actual practice in the field.

But it is hoped that the following **general hints** will be helpful in making your programming interviews more effective. These suggestions are culled from the experiences of agents who have been outstandingly successful in program selling.

The Approach

Ask "lead" questions. "Are your policies lapse-proof?" (Automatic Premium Loan Clause). "Could bill collectors seize your family's insurance money?" (Spendthrift Clause). "Have you disinherited any children?" (Beneficiary Arrangements). "What happens to your insurance if you become seriously disabled?" (Waiver of Premium Clause). Such questions seldom fail to get attention and interest.

Show examples of your service. You might use your own program, or work up a typical "John Doe" case. Explain how the proper coordination of assets will increase substantially the values of existing life insurance. Include in your display kit a number of letters of appreciation from well-satisfied (and preferably well-known) clients in your community.

Set the stage. When calling in the home don't hesitate to ask for help in creating the atmosphere for your interview. When a prospect **serves** you, you become a **guest** toward whom he or she feels more friendly. Ask where to put your coat—ask for more light—ask to have the TV turned down or off—ask to use a **table.** Many agents prefer the informal atmosphere of the **kitchen or dining table,** where the family is accustomed to talking over its problems.

Fact-finding

What facts should be obtained? Frequently, the prospects' policies are not at hand for inspection. Even when they are, many agents prefer not to get involved in the details of policy analysis—at least not in the initial stages of the programming interview.

They want to determine, first, whether:

a. prospects have needs that are not covered,
b. they are concerned about their problems,

c. **they can and will put aside some money to remedy the situation and**
d. **there is anyone else from whom they are committed to buy.**

If the object, then, is to find out whether you have a real prospect or a mere suspect, you will want to make a quick estimate of the prospect's insurance requirements and match these against his or her present assets to see if there is a deficiency. For quick figuring, you will need only a few facts about each of the prospect's policies:

- The company
- The face amount
- The kind of policy
- The year of issue

This information often will suffice for more elaborate planning at the office, with the use of one of the several settlement option manuals available.

Learn family names. Quickly become familiar with names of persons your prospects love. For whom do they work so hard? Whose security do they worry about? Who would suffer most if they died? Motivation **begins** with the first mention of their names. So, **learn** the names. **Use** them throughout your interviews in place of such impersonal terms as "your children" or "your son" or "your daughter." How much more effective to talk of "shoes for Johnny"—"dresses for Susan"!

Which comes first—needs or assets? Some agents prefer to determine survivor and retirement needs before questioning prospects about their assets. They say that prospects will be reluctant to reveal such personal information—**unless** they understand what use is to be made of it.

It's a matter of choice, but it may be more practical to determine assets first, for this good reason: **When you know the types and amount of assets, you are in a far better position to obtain down-to-earth estimates of cash and income needs later in your interviews.** If families are to be on a "hamburger" budget, it's best to know it before you cater to "porterhouse steak" appetites. Hesitancy of prospects to reveal their financial status is perfectly normal. **You can anticipate and overcome that attitude by first giving your prospects valuable information.** For example, you can tell them about the thousands of dollars in Social Security benefits that are earmarked for them and their families.

Encourage adequate (not minimum) income. Social Security benefits do not provide a decent standard of living for the family in the large majority of cases. But the altitude of benefits is such that the old "minimum income" concept has been killed off. It used to be standard procedure to ask, "What's the **least** your family can get along on?" But now, with Social Security benefits so high, there's a danger of "minimizing" yourself right out of a sale. **Instead, you can guide the prospect in specifying a family income which is adequate, comfortable, and more nearly related to present living standards.** Appeal to their pride. Help them elevate their sights.

What to do with liquid assets. Assets other than life insurance can be troublesome in programming, yet they can't be ignored, for two reasons: (a) **Prospects take pride in their ownership.** After they have scrimped and saved to build up a bank account or buy government bonds, they want their efforts to be admired—not disregarded. (b) **Assets that are definite in value and liquid in nature have a place in the program.** They can be used to meet cash needs, thereby freeing life insurance proceeds for the job of providing income. Assets of this kind would include money in checking and savings accounts, savings and loan shares, and U.S. Government bonds.

It is difficult to convert liquid assets into guaranteed income for the family. So it is advisable to allocate such assets to various cash needs. The final expense block is a good place to write off liquid assets. Of course, if the assets are earning a fair rate of interest, they may be held as an emergency fund, without forcing a surviving spouse to cash them in at once. **The point is that liquid assets should be absorbed by one or more of the cash needs** so they will not clutter up the income portions of the program.

Quickly match assets against needs. As stated previously, many agents proceed rapidly to show prospects that they have a deficiency. Then they are in a position to motivate them into doing something about it. It has been suggested, too, that liquid assets be allocated to cash needs. As for the "spending" of present insurance, **it is practical and sensible to lump all policies together,** regardless of kind or settlement option guarantees, adding all face amounts to arrive at a total for quick analysis.

Of course this "lumping" procedure is **not** recommended for finished programming, wherein settlement option interest rates are analyzed carefully and policies allocated to produce the largest possible values.

But in the process of quickly analyzing existing programs of prospects, agents can write off needs with dollars taken from a common fund of life insurance proceeds. For example, an agent can dip into the fund and pay off the mortgage or set up an emergency fund or take care of any other cash need—then use the balance to show an amount of monthly income for the Dependency Period at whatever level the residue will provide. With all assets expected, and with needs left uncovered, the agent is well on the way toward making a sale of new insurance.

Talk in terms of income rather than face amounts. When prospects think in terms of the BIG face amounts printed on the front of their policies, they have the tendency to say, "I'm loaded" or "I'm insurance poor."

So quickly pass over face amounts and convert them into the terms of monthly income. "Your ABC policy will provide $300 a month until Johnny is through high school." "Your XYZ policy will put $200 into Ms. Prospect's purse each month until her old-age Social Security income starts."

Nothing will bring prospects down to earth quite so fast as the interpretation of face amounts into the language of monthly income. It's simply good selling procedure and a vital part of good programming technique.

Get a definite commitment. A "commitment" can mean any number of things, depending on the agent's attitude and training. But every good life insurance agent will insist on getting prospects to take some **positive action** in the first interview.

It's an excellent idea to make a list of possible commitments, from the strongest to the weakest. Then, in the interview, you can **strive for the most emphatic commitment,** backing off to less positive ones only when necessary to secure the prospect's cooperation. The following list is an example, although the commitments may not be exactly in the order you prefer:

- Signed application with deposit
- Signed application, no deposit
- Verbal commitment to buy
- Commitment to pay a certain amount
- Interest in seeing a completed program or proposal
- Definite date for another interview
- Securing of referred leads
- Will buy from YOU when ready

The point is that **unless the interview results in some definite progress toward a sale, it is time wasted.** And life insurance agents cannot afford to waste time. **Time is their capital.** If a mutually profitable relationship cannot be established with a prospect, it is best to find this out quickly, thereby conserving irreplaceable time for better prospects. Commitments are GO signs in your progress toward a sale. Lack of commitments are STOP signs, and it's a waste of time to be at a standstill.

The Solution

First things first. To most agents, the procedure of "first things first" is so thoroughly ingrained that mention of it may seem superfluous. Yet you will still find agents who sell fine educational programs, while the family is left without adequate income until the children are of college age. Or the insured has been induced to give greater importance to retirement needs than to the bread-and-butter needs of the family. In many cases thought has been given to family income without provisions for clearing the mortgage, leaving some doubt as to whether the family will have a mailbox into which their monthly checks can be dropped.

Of course, the agent is not always entirely at fault. Some prospects **insist** on having certain later needs satisfied first. The agent either carries out the prospect's wishes or loses a sale. **But in the process of earning a commission, the agent should make the picture clear.**

Just as a refresher, here is a checklist of family and retirement needs in the usually accepted order of "first things first":

- **Cash for final expenses.** All bills and taxes must be paid to give the family a clean start on its new budget.
- **Mortgage cancellation.** The family's housing situation directly affects income requirements. It's much more economical to pay off the principal in cash, rather than saddle the family with monthly payments on principal AND interest.
- **Emergency fund and/or adjustment income.** A reserve of cash to meet unforeseeable expenses that would wreck the family's budget. Also reduces the shock of a drop to a lower income level if part of the fund is paid out in installments over a short period.
- **Dependency period income.** Enough income so that a parent can stay home and take care of the children while they are young, so that he or she won't be forced to work and lose Social Security benefits.
- **Life income for the widow.** A check each month so she will be financially independent at the time when the children are establishing their homes and getting started in their careers.
- **Education.** Funds, guaranteed to be available whether Dad lives or dies, for children's college education or special training. A college education today is almost a **must** for many children, if they

are to have the best of opportunities for happiness and success.

- **Retirement income.** Guaranteed, lifelong income to supplement and protect Social Security—enough income to permit Dad and Mom to get along independently of the children. Disability statistics show that Americans have a three to seven chance of becoming disabled between the ages 30 and 65. Those in this group are twice as likely to have a long-term disability as facing the possibility of death. Yet, many agents omit special efforts in selling products to meet this need.

Seldom will you find prospects with the premium paying ability to take care of all these needs adequately. So in almost every case you will have to apply the rule of "first things first." This will give you daily opportunities to convince prospects of your sincere interest in their situations and of your desire to be of real service.

Proper distribution of policy proceeds. More often than not a prospect will have an assortment of life insurance policies, some old and some new. **As a general rule, the older policies will contain more favorable settlement option rates** than those guaranteed under newer policies and under the insurance you are proposing. And if there is a group insurance policy, there may be restrictions on paying it out over a period of years.

So, it is usually good practice to use group insurance and new insurance for immediate cash needs. Every effort must be made to conserve policies with high-interest options for income purposes.

Be careful in proposing decreasing term. Pure decreasing term insurance and family income policies have enjoyed great popularity. When the prospect can scrape up very little money for new premiums, the tendency has been to load the program with decreasing term in one form or another, so that the insured will have the most protection for the least outlay.

This is sound procedure so long as the insured's family has a need for additional income during the Dependency Period or a mortgage that needs to be paid off. But the procedure may be decidedly unsound when the new insurance is bought to provide for a deficiency in the later years, for example during the Blackout Period. The commuted value of the proposed insurance decreases every year, so if the insured lives for 5, 10, 15 or 20 years there is less and less likelihood that enough insurance will be available to do the job outlined.

So, when decreasing term is used, the agent **must check to make sure that the total insurance re-**

maining will be sufficient to meet family income objectives—**no matter when the insured dies.**

Work out alternative solutions. It is good sales technique to have these alternatives at your fingertips, regardless of whether you are using the one-interview or two-interview sales procedure. We have said that it's unusual to find a prospect with the premium-paying ability to provide adequately for all needs—cash, family income and retirement. Unless the prospect gives you a definite dollar commitment, **it's wise to outline, first, a program that you feel is somewhat beyond the prospect's reach.** Then you have some leeway in cutting back the program to the extent

CAUTION

It may be unwise to put a number of solutions side by side and expect prospects to decide which one to buy. Usually they're having trouble enough trying to decide whether to buy at all—or whether to put their money into a new car, freezer, TV or whatever. Further choices may make them even more uncertain in their minds.

In an interview, show the one solution you think is best. Produce another only when necessary to keep the case alive.

necessary to bring the premium within the prospect's means. This is the same technique employed by the clothing salesperson in showing the most expensive suit or dress first. It's flattering: there is always the chance that the customer can afford more than was originally estimated, and it's far easier to come down than go up in price.

There are three methods of reducing premium outlay:

a. **lowering the benefits,** without shortening the period over which they are paid,
b. **cutting off family income in later years,** without reducing benefits in the earlier years of the program and
c. **dropping from higher-premium to lower-premium insurance,** without reducing benefits or eliminating later periods of income.

The accepted solution may even be a combination of these methods.

Of course, prospects must make the final decision as to **how much** and **where** to cut the program. But it is your responsibility to help them in their thinking, using as your guide the rule of "first things first."

Make solutions neat and attractive. Many agents prefer to sell on a one-interview basis. Their solutions are worked out on the spot, and the prospect either accepts them or rejects them.

Others prefer to end the first interview at the conclusion of the fact-finding procedure, then call back after preparing a graph, chart or other type of proposal for the prospect's consideration. For those who adhere to this technique, **the following suggestions may be helpful:**

- **Be neat.** Remember, your proposal represents you. An attractive proposal indicates that you are careful, efficient, and reliable—that you are concerned about the prospect's problems and have given very serious thought to them. It also shows the kind of continued service the prospect can expect from you.
- **Be accurate.** Use care in preparing your figures, for all of the reasons above. Then too, if a mistake becomes apparent, the prospect may doubt the soundness of your whole proposition.
- **Personalize.** Instead of "wife" and "child," show actual names so that the insurance benefits are quickly related to those the prospect loves most. Especially display the prospect's own name prominently, using an attractive personalized folder, if possible. Prospects will appreciate your efforts in developing **tailor-made programs—just for them.**

> Organize your dreams, and they'll organize you—*Sidney Friedman*

- **Use color,** if you can. Color adds much to the attractiveness and clarity of a programming chart. For example, one color for Social Security, another for present insurance, and a third for proposed new insurance will enable the prospect to understand and appreciate quickly (1) the benefits of the new insurance, (2) its relationship to the prospect's other assets and (3) the quality of your service in combining all assets so that they produce the utmost income and work together as a harmonious team.

The Close

Review the first interview. The suggestion refers only to agents who consider it preferable or expedient to close on a second interview, after working out a solution at home or back at the office.

When a case has developed to the solution stage, it is likely that certain objectives were successfully accomplished in the first interview, such as:

a. revealing the needs of the prospect,

b. pointing out the deficiency of present assets with respect to meeting those needs and
c. motivating the prospect to the extent that he or she appears willing to do something about the problem.

But so very often "hot" prospects tend to cool off in the interval between the first and second interviews. Their minds become occupied with day-to-day problems and, as the first-interview motivation wears off, it may well be that their desire to satisfy **current** needs will grow stronger than their intentions to provide security for the future. **So it is usually necessary to "warm up" prospects again** by going back over the points made and the conclusions reached during the first interview.

In resetting the stage, it is advisable to review briefly the worksheets used in the first interview—the same graph, chart, or fact-finding sheet on which the prospect's needs were originally illustrated. The object is to renew the problems in prospects' minds and remotivate them through the same stimuli that caused them to react favorably in the initial interview.

- How much do I have to take out of my pocket?
- What goes back into my pocket if I live?
- What does my family get out of it if I die?
- What happens to my money if I can't keep making payments?

Avoid face amounts and technical terms. In explaining your solution, remember that the prospect is primarily concerned about the answers to these questions:

Although the life value of your prospect and needs for future income are represented by thousands of dollars, the prospect's **thinking is geared to weekly or monthly amounts** of income and outgo. Prospects may be shocked and repelled by your emphasizing a need for $50,000, $75,000 or $100,000 of insurance. How much more effective to present your solution **in terms of—**

- The size of the checks it will produce.
- The regularity with which they will arrive in the mail.
- The long period of time they will be available to pay for food, clothing and shelter.

Surveys show that the buying public is greatly confused by technical life insurance terms. So **keep your explanation simple—talk the prospect's language,** not the language of rate books. Don't say "double indemnity"—say "If you are killed accidentally, your wife will receive **twice** as much." Don't refer to "settlement options"—explain how the money will be (or can be) paid over the years. Don't say "waiver of premium"—say "if you become sick or disabled so that you can't work anymore, we'll make premium payments for you. When you get well, you won't owe us a cent!"

The person who **understands** the tremendous values of life insurance is the person who **buys** insurance—**and keeps it!**

Be careful of rigid settlement arrangements. Although the setting up of rigid settlement options may be desirable in some cases, in other instances the procedure may be unsatisfactory, even **dangerous.**

For example, policies might be designated to take care of consecutive income periods, with settlement options arranged accordingly. If the insured subsequently lapsed one or more policies, the surviving spouse **could be left with an erratic income program.**

Or a program might be set up that appears adequate in light of **today's** cost of living. So proceeds are spread "thin" by settlement options over a long period of time. **Here, the surviving spouse might find the income ridiculously low in relation to increased costs and a higher economic level** to which the family has become accustomed. Although there might be a crying need to convert some of the future income into present income the beneficiary and the insurance companies would be helpless to do anything about it.

Many agents suggest that clients keep programs flexible by applying the interest option to all or at least some of their policies. Then they guide insured spouses in drawing up letters of instruction to their husbands or wives, advising them as to the selection of appropriate settlement options for the various cash and income needs. The letter represents current best thinking on the subject, but it recognizes that **tomorrow's** unforeseen conditions might justify changes in the plan.

It is obvious that there can be **no standard rule governing the application of settlement options.** The facts of each individual case must be considered. The best the agent can do is to point out the advantages and disadvantages of setting up a flexible or a rigid program—**and then carry out the client's instructions to the letter.**

Give all service promised. Many agents use a "service" approach in getting the interest of prospects and in inducing them to reveal the necessary facts about their situations. Unfortunately, some underwriters have been guilty of forgetting or sidestepping this promise, once the sale has been made. Needless to say, this practice undermines the prestige of the agent and is a reflection on our profession.

So, if you agree to bring beneficiary clauses up to date—coordinate the settlement options—adjust the premium schedule—add the desirable protection provisions—**you have a job to do!**

> When you sell a service, you assume a moral obligation to your client, your company, your fellow underwriters. You are pledged to complete every detail of service promised.

Provide a lasting service. A program is like a snapshot. It represents the client's situation as of **the moment the picture is taken.** But the program is subject to constant change—changes in assets, in family status, in needs and attitudes. **So a program just completed is a job just begun.**

That is the marvelous advantage of program selling. You create a **job** of taking care of the client. **Your job grows as your client grows in financial stature.** Consistent service gives your job a **permanency.** Add a job here, a job there—and soon you have a **career.** In short, a conscientious and continuous service **builds clientele, produces high-quality leads, brings substantial repeat business, and leads to a self-satisfying, highly paid, secure career in life underwriting.**

8

Estate Protection

An easy-to-read, easy-to-understand introduction to estate protection—for the underwriter who wants to know what this field of activity is all about.

Here is a summary of the steps in estate planning—an explanation of the problems of estate conservation, and solutions—a brief description of the essential features and purposes of instruments used in effective estate distribution. This section can be a springboard to further, more intensive study of the subject.

> Let me show you what part of your estate isn't yours—*Ben Feldman*

WHAT IS ESTATE PLANNING?

It has been pointed out that the line of separation between package selling and total needs selling, or programming as it is sometimes called, is indistinct. Similarly, there is no definite dividing line between total needs selling and estate planning. Total needs selling deals mainly with a client's life insurance estate and the coordination of life insurance with a few other assets such as Social Security and holdings of a liquid nature. The transition from total needs selling to estate planning occurs at some uncertain point where the client's other assets are of significant proportions and the size of the estate is such that appreciable settlement costs and death taxes can be anticipated. Estate planning per se, however, is necessarily handled by an estate planning team, which generally includes a lawyer, accountant, life underwriter, and sometimes a trust officer.

So far as the **objectives** of total needs selling and estate planning are concerned, they are practically identical: (1) **conservation** of the largest possible portion of the estate in the process of its passing to the heirs and (2) **distribution** of the estate in the most efficient manner consistent with the estate owner's desires of providing for the heirs. But in achieving these objectives, estate planners must analyze the client's **entire holdings,** including life insurance, and bring all property into harmonious arrangement for the maximum benefit of the estate owner and the family.

Of course, a complete discussion of estate planning cannot be condensed into these few pages. But the following outline will give the underwriter an understanding of the **scope** of estate planning, the problems involved, and the various settlement arrangements that are available for solving these problems. If you are not yet familiar with the various aspects of estate protection, it is hoped that our brief treatment will whet your appetite for further study and induce you to investigate this very lucrative area of sales activity and counseling service.

STEPS IN ESTATE PLANNING

First Step—Assembling of Facts

A. **Material resources**—a complete list of all assets possessed by the estate owner and other family members.

B. **Personal family data**—facts regarding age, relationship, health, etc., concerning each family member.

C. **Objectives**—desires of estate owner with respect to providing for the heirs, preserving or liquidating business interest, making bequests, etc.

Second Step—Analysis of Facts

A. **Analysis of property**
   1. Items passing into the executor's hands by **kind of property** (cash or equivalent; items to be converted into cash; items to be distributed in kind) and by **tax status** (items qualifying for marital deduction; items that do not qualify).
   2. Items passing outside the probate estate by reason of survivorship title or under terms of contract.

B. **Estimate of debts, claims, expenses and taxes**
   1. Assuming husband dies first.
   2. Assuming wife dies first.

C. **Determination of suitability of property**
   1. To cover the needs for cash.
   2. To provide adequate income for those who will need it as long as they will need it.

D. **Searching out defects in present settlement arrangements**

E. **Exposing technical defects in present instruments of transfer and disposition**

Third Step—Selection of Plan

A. **Formulating the best plan** to meet all objectives of the estate owner
B. **Testing the plan** by once again simulating the procedure of administration at estate owner's death
C. **Final selection of the plan,** including all component methods of transfer and disposition

Fourth Step—Execution of the Plan

A. **Drawing up all necessary instruments by an attorney,** perhaps with the cooperation of a trust officer
B. **Taking all necessary personal and legal actions**

Fifth Step—Periodic Review and Revision

A. **Changes in personal and financial circumstances**
B. **Changes in applicable laws**

The two major objectives of estate planning, **effective conservation** and **proper distribution,** are the analyst's guideposts in every step of the planning procedure. Now we shall examine the problems of conservation and the methods of distribution.

ESTATE CONSERVATION

An estate must pass through the hands of other people before it reaches the heirs. During this period of transfer, the estate may suffer severe losses arising from settlement costs and forced liquidation of assets. Therefore, the first steps in planning an estate are:

- to analyze the causes of shrinkage;
- to minimize them as much as possible; and
- to provide cash with which to pay costs that cannot be eliminated or further reduced.

COSTS OF ESTATE SETTLEMENT

Funeral and Administration Expenses: During the period of estate transfer, control of the estate is placed in the hands of either an executor (appointed by the deceased in his or her will) or an administrator (who, in the absence of a will, is appointed by and responsible to the court).

The executor or administrator must pay funeral expenses and perform many complex duties of a legal and accounting nature, all resulting in appreciable costs that are chargeable to the estate. The tables on pages 168 and 169 shows the average debts and administration costs for estates of various sizes.

TABLE OF AVERAGE ESTATE DEBTS

	Total Debts	
Gross Estate	*Amount*	*Percent*
$ 50,000	$ 2,900	5.8
75,000	4,300	5.7
100,000	5,600	5.6
150,000	8,250	5.5
200,000	10,600	5.3
250,000	13,000	5.2
300,000	15,600	5.2
400,000	20,400	5.1
500,000	25,000	5.0
750,000	35,250	4.7
1,000,000	45,000	4.5
2,000,000	82,000	4.1
3,000,000	120,000	4.0
5,000,000	185,000	3.7

Debts: The executor or administrator is also directed to pay the deceased's debts—all the many things the estate owner bought or was obligated to buy and had not yet paid for at death. The term "debts" includes, too, all taxes (personal property, real estate and income) that have accrued to the date of death).

These charges also take an appreciable bite out of the estate, as illustrated in the table on page 169. Here

TABLE OF ESTIMATED ADMINISTRATION COSTS

	Administration Expense	
Gross Estate	*Amount*	*Percent*
$ 50,000	$ 2,300	4.6
75,000	3,450	4.6
100,000	4,600	4.6
150,000	6,900	4.6
200,000	9,200	4.6
250,000	11,500	4.6
300,000	13,800	4.6
400,000	18,400	4.6
500,000	22,500	4.5
750,000	33,000	4.4
1,000,000	43,000	4.3
2,000,000	84,000	4.2
3,000,000	126,000	4.2

we have used the same reports concerning the estates mentioned previously.

Federal estate tax: Since 1931, the top federal estate tax bracket has gone up from 20 percent to 70 percent. As of 1993, the maximum transfer tax rate is 50 percent for transfers in excess of $2.5 million.

WILLS OFTEN NEGLECTED

Questionnaires mailed to thousands of Columbia University alumni—physicians, lawyers, dentists, engineers, pharmacists, educators—revealed the astonishing fact that in some of these intelligent categories as few as 18½ percent had wills.

—From *What Happens When a Man Dies?* by Donald G. Dutcher, Surrogate, Bergen County, New Jersey

On the other hand, some measure of relief has been granted through the marital deduction privilege. Effective with the passage of the Economic Recovery Tax Act of 1981, this deduction, which is unlimited, allows a decedent to pass qualifying property to his or her surviving spouse free of federal estate tax. But in spite of this relief, proper estate planning is still vital to assure sufficient liquidity and to guarantee that the estate owner's wishes are fulfilled.

State death taxes: Every state imposes some kind of death tax, an inheritance tax or an estate tax or both. These taxes must be given careful consideration in moderate as well as large estates because they contribute substantially to estate shrinkage.

Losses due to forced liquidation. Administration, costs, debts and taxes are direct charges against the estate. Liquidation losses are not in the same category, but they are closely related to settlement costs and have the same effect of disastrous depreciation of the estate.

Most debts and administration costs must be paid within the first year; most estate and inheritance taxes are due in nine months. Payment of these costs requires liquid assets, of which the average estate has less than 10 percent.

Often there is a **double** loss: (1) property is sold at a loss and (2) the heirs lose all future income that might have been derived from the property!

MINIMIZING SETTLEMENT COSTS

Preparation of a will: A well-planned will, drawn by a lawyer, enables an estate owner to name an executor, lay out a complete and detailed program of action for the executor to follow, grant him or her the powers necessary to carry out instructions and eliminate the expense of a bond. The executor can operate more promptly and effectively, thus reducing the costs of estate administration. By comparison, the efforts of an administrator are cumbersome. The administrator can act only within the confines of statutory provisions, and it is likely that the procedure

UNIFIED FEDERAL GIFT AND ESTATE TAX*

Taxable Gift or Estate		Tentative Tax	
Col. 1 From	To	Tax on Col. 1	Rate on Excess
$ 0	$ 10,000	$ 0	18%
10,000	20,000	1,800	20
20,000	40,000	3,800	22
40,000	60,000	8,200	24
60,000	80,000	13,000	26
80,000	100,000	18,200	28
100,000	150,000	23,800	30
150,000	250,000	38,800	32
250,000	500,000	70,800	34
500,000	750,000	155,800	37
750,000	1,000,000	248,300	39
1,000,000	1,250,000	345,800	41

Taxable Gift or Estate		Tentative Tax	
Col. 1 From	To	Tax on Col. 1	Rate on Excess
$1,250,000	$1,500,000	$ 448,300	43%
1,500,000	2,000,000	555,800	45
2,000,000	2,500,000	780,800	49
2,500,000	Infinity	1,025,800	50

*There is a possibility that the 55% prior top rate will be restored in 1993.

Gift and Estate Tax Credit†

Unified Credit	Tax-Sheltered Estate
$192,800	$600,000

†If any portion of the old $30,000 gift tax exemption was used for gifts made after September 8, 1976 and before January 1, 1977, then the gift and estate tax credit is reduced by 20 percent of the exemption so used. For example, if the entire $30,000 exemption was used for a gift made on October 15, 1976, the $192,800 credit would be reduced by $6,000 (20 percent of $30,000). Also, the benefit of the unified credit for estates over $10 million is phased out by a 5 percent surcharge on transfers between $10 million and $18,340,000.

of administration will be drawn out and far more costly.

The estate tax marital deduction: After the will, the estate tax marital deduction is often the next thing considered by the estate planner, for in many estates, the federal estate tax is the largest single contributor to estate shrinkage. And the estate tax marital deduction is the single most important arrangement for offsetting this shrinkage. Its enactment in 1948 caused a revolution in estate planning and it has since become a key arrangement in most estate plans.

The estate tax marital deduction is only available if the estate owner is survived by his or her spouse. The estate owner is permitted to transfer to the surviving spouse an unlimited amount of property free of federal estate tax. Of course, the property must be includible in the decedent's gross estate.

To qualify property for the marital deduction, it must be left to the spouse outright or in such a manner that the surviving spouse has the right, at least, to dispose of it as he or she sees fit at death. An estate does not qualify automatically for the marital deduction. Care must be taken by the planner to see that the assets intended to qualify for the marital deduction do so qualify.

It should be remembered, of course, that when property is left to a spouse in such manner that it qualifies for the marital deduction and remains in the spouse's estate, it is subject to federal estate tax at the death of the spouse.

A single unified rate schedule for calculating both estate and gift taxes was established by the Tax Reform Act of 1976. The rates are progressive on the basis of cumulative lifetime and deathtime transfers.

The annual gift tax exclusion is $10,000. Gift splitting by spouses to third parties, e.g., a $20,000 annual exclusion per donee, if both spouses agree on the gift to a third party, is also available.

Gift tax marital deduction: A gift tax marital deduction has been allowed in one form or another since April 3, 1948.

The current gift tax marital deduction, like the estate marital deduction, is unlimited. That is, any amount can be transferred from one spouse to another without giving rise to a gift tax.

It should also be noted that the annual gift tax exclusion is now $10,000 ($20,000 for spousal gifts), which would enable the estate owner to establish a generous schedule of annual premiums (gifts) to any number of donees.

Business buy-sell agreements: The estate owner may be a partner in a business firm or a stockholder of a close corporation. In such a case, there are many advantages of a binding agreement whereby the surviving business associates agree to buy, and the estate owner agrees to sell at death, his or her interest at a price mutually agreed upon as satisfactory.

However, we are concerned for the moment only with the particular advantage of savings in the federal estate tax.

When a business owner dies, his or her interest passes to the estate and becomes subject to the estate tax. In the absence of a properly drawn buy-sell agreement, it is quite likely that the Commissioner will set a value on the interest (with special emphasis on the valuation of goodwill) considerably higher than the value estimated by the executor. The tax must be paid on this "increased" value unless the estate takes the case to court. Even then it is probable that the court will increase the value materially over the amount the executor contends should be taxed.

But when the value of the business interest is set forth in a buy-sell agreement (containing certain well-defined provisions which make it acceptable), the stipulated value will apply for federal estate tax purposes. Thus, the tax will be held to a minimum.

Life insurance beneficiary arrangements: When life insurance proceeds are made payable to named beneficiaries, the death benefits pass outside of probate. Consequently, administration costs are saved. Also, state death taxes are usually reduced or eliminated. It may be, too, no federal estate tax will apply to the proceeds. This is the case if the insured had no incidents of ownership in the policy.

PROVISION OF CASH TO PAY ESTATE SETTLEMENT COSTS

It has been pointed out that the average estate is less than 10 percent liquid, while the percentage of estate settlement costs run much higher. And these costs must be paid quickly and in cash. Life insurance is the only adequate answer to the perplexing problem of estate liquidity, for the following reasons:

1. **Life insurance provides the cash needed exactly when needed.** The death that creates the need simultaneously provides the liquidity. There is no need to tie up cash or liquid securities, and no need to establish a sinking fund, even if there were time to do so.
2. **Life insurance can be adjusted to meet anticipated costs.** As the estate grows, and the expected settlement costs grow with it, the amount of life

insurance can be increased. Or, if the estate grows smaller, policies can be split or shifted to provide for other needs. This flexibility is unique in life insurance.

3. **Life insurance avoids a forced sale of estate assets.** Estate values are preserved and income retained for the heirs. Funds are provided **for** the estate—not **from** the estate.
4. **Life insurance reduces administration costs.** The simpler the process of settlement, the smaller the administration costs. When there is ample cash on hand and no need to resort to forced liquidation, the executor can administer the estate quickly and efficiently.
5. **Life insurance can be removed from the insured's taxable estate.** The estate owner can buy life insurance to provide estate liquidity, relinquish all ownership in the policy, even continue to make premium payments, and **keep the proceeds out of his or her taxable estate.** (Life insurance trusts, for the achievement of this purpose, are discussed on page 187.)
6. **Life insurance ideally supports a business agreement.** A buy-sell agreement can eliminate a forced sale of the deceased's business interest at distress prices and transfer the full value of the interest to the heirs. In most cases the only prac-

tical and possible way to back up the agreement is through life insurance.

7. **Life insurance makes funds available at a discount.** The estate can buy liquidity dollars at a few cents annually on the dollar. Especially in the early years of the policy, life insurance provides greater returns in estate dollars for every dollar invested than does any other kind of plan or property.

SURVIVORSHIP LIFE—"SECOND-TO-DIE" CONTRACTS

In recent years, surivorship life insurance, or "second-to-die" policies, have found increasing use in estate plan life sales. This type of life insurance can provide an economical and effective method to obviate the necessity of invading the estate to pay taxes. The unique feature of this policy is that two lives are insured under one contract and the insurance benefit is paid only upon the death of the second person insured. This is usually when the largest estate tax bill becomes due.

This type of sale is more applicable to the upscale prospect. Some statistics show that the average amount of coverage sold under survivorship contracts is above the million dollar mark. While the majority of sales are to married couples, survivorship life is used in corporate situations, for example in insuring key personnel. There are also useful applications in split-dollar plans and charitable remainder trusts.

Other advantages are built into this imaginatively designed policy contract. In survivorship life plans, a large increase in cash values and in dividends often occurs at the death of the first insured. Policy loan options can serve as a source for emergency cash to meet final expenses such as burial, debt clearance and payment of state death taxes. Some plans also provide substantial increases in cash values starting from the early policy years and often exceeding the amount of annual payments, thus making "vanishing premium" options available. Fifth dividend options are also offered, adding an increasing death benefit to the face amount of the policy, which can provide a built-in hedge against escalating taxes as estate values increase through the years.

As in other estate tax insurance transactions, ownership arrangements are important in survivorship life purchases. Designation of ownership should avoid inclusion of the insurance proceeds in the insured's estate. Having a trustee apply for, pay the premiums on, and own the policy is a practical arrangement and can help avoid a possible contemplation of death attribution by the Internal Revenue Service.

While paying taxes through the purchase of life insurance has always been less expensive than paying full dollar amounts from the estate, survivorship life costs make the product even more attractive. For example, a 50-year-old client with a $3.5 million estate could purchase a survivorship policy with a $60,000 annual premium for about a six- or seven-year period in order to pay off the estate tax obligation. Without the insurance in the picture, the legator would have to virtually double the size of the estate at death, in order to leave his or her beneficiaries the identical after-tax gifts; or to look at it another way, suppose a client with a $6 million estate faces an estate tax of $3 million. If the premium for $3 million of life insurance is $280,000, that figure represents about a 93 percent discount on the tax bill.

ESTATE DISTRIBUTION

Undue emphasis must not be placed on minimizing death taxes and settlement costs. The primary purpose of estate planning is to **provide for the welfare of the family.** Considerations of tax and cost reductions are important only to the extent that they achieve maximum family benefits consistent with the estate owner's objectives of safety, security, and proper apportionment of the property.

In outlining the following instruments and methods of estate distribution, we shall continue to point out the potential savings in taxes and administration costs. However, we do not infer that one means of distribution is better than another merely because of such savings. Many other factors are involved, **and the estate owner's desires for the family are paramount.**

Our aim, here, is simply to present a brief description of the essential features and purposes of the tools most commonly used in estate distribution. A far more comprehensive study of these techniques must be undertaken before an agent can be qualified to apply them to field activities. Even then, the details of most of these procedures must be left up to an attorney or trust officer.

THE WILL

Essential Features: A will is the basic instrument in estate settlement arrangements. It may be defined as "a legal declaration of a person's intention or wish regarding what shall be done after his or her death touching the disposition of property, the guardianship of children or the administration of the estate."

The **testator** (maker) must be "of age," according to statute. Generally, to be valid, the will must be written, signed and witnessed by the required number of witnesses under the state law. An **executor** is the person named by the estate owner in the will as the one to settle the estate. A **codicil** is a paper intended as a supplement or addition to an existing will, to effect some revision or change.

Purposes: In addition to naming an executor, the will permits the estate owner to delegate the powers necessary to administration, eliminate the expense of a bond, pass property to those selected heirs in the proportions desired, specify which property is to be used for what purposes, and coordinate the provisions that govern property passing under the will with the provisions made through other instruments.

If the estate owner dies **intestate** (without having made a valid will), the decedent's property is distributed among heirs according to state law, regardless of any wishes or plans the decedent might have had concerning distribution.

LIFE INSURANCE SETTLEMENT ARRANGEMENTS

Essential Features: It is assumed that every underwriter is familiar with options under which life insurance proceeds (or annuities) may be paid out: **cash; interest only,** with payment of proceeds deferred; payment over a **specified period,** at whatever level of income the proceeds will provide; payment of **a specified income** as long as the proceeds and interest will last; and the various **life income** and **joint and survivorship** arrangements. Such options may be selected by the insured, or the insured may prefer that the beneficiary select the option or combination of options that will be most practical.

Beneficiary designations may be **revocable** (can be changed at will) or **irrevocable** (can be changed only with beneficiary's consent). And, the proceeds may be split among a number of beneficiaries.

Purposes: The estate owner's main purpose in using life insurance (or annuity) settlement arrangements is self-evident—**to distribute the proceeds to whomever, in whatever amounts, and over whatever period of time he or she chooses.** Or, these choices may be extended to the beneficiary. By combinations of the options, the estate owner has considerable flexibility in working out the desired plan of distribution.

There are additional advantages in life insurance arrangements that may not be quite so apparent. These include **savings in administration costs** when proceeds pass directly to beneficiaries instead of going through the executor's hands. This arrangement also usually results in **savings in state death taxes,** and it will **eliminate federal estate tax** on proceeds if the estate owner does not own the contract (assuming the "contemplation of death" rule does not apply) and the proceeds are not payable to his or her estate.

If the widow is the beneficiary, the settlement options offer her an **income tax advantage.** Except for the interest only option, when proceeds are paid periodically over a period of time, part of each payment represents a return of principal (face amount) and part represents an interest payment. No beneficiary is required to pay income tax on the return of principal portion, as only the interest portion is taxable.

Life insurance proceeds may be arranged to **qualify for the marital deduction** by naming the widow beneficiary and specifying that her estate is to receive any unpaid balance at her death. Or, contingent beneficiaries may be named if the widow is given the power to eliminate them and substitute any other disposition of the remainder. A popular **nonqualified** arrangement is to pay the widow interest only (although payments of principal can be set up, too) with the unpaid balance going to one or more contingent beneficiaries.

TESTAMENTARY TRUSTS

Essential Features: A testamentary trust may be created by the estate owner's will. The trust instrument (which is incorporated in the terms of the will) designates the trustee, specifies the property to be put in trust, names the beneficiary(ies) of the trust, gives instructions as to investments and distribution of trust income, and specifies when and to whom the trust property is ultimately to be delivered. The trust passes through the hands of the executor and is subject to the probate court.

Purposes: The testamentary trust is frequently used to relieve beneficiaries of management worries and financial responsibilities. **Trust property is put into the hands of persons who have experience and skill** in property management, investments, accounting and tax matters. Such services are especially valuable when minor or legally incompetent beneficiaries are involved, or where the widow or widower is incapable of handling the financial affairs of the family. Explicit instructions may be given the trustee concerning investments and disbursements of money to beneficiaries. Sometimes the trustee is permitted to exercise judgment under certain conditions. Frequently, the arrangement is extremely flexible, with the trustee having unlimited discretion in matters of investments and income payments to beneficiaries.

For tax purposes, the estate owner may wish to create two testamentary trusts. Under one trust, the widow is left property **which qualifies for the**

marital deduction. She has the right to enjoy the income from this "marital trust" and either draw upon the trust principal during her life or dispose of it as she sees fit at her death. Property remaining in the "marital trust" will be taxable in her estate. The second ("nonmarital") trust will include property that is designated to go to someone else (usually the children) at the wife's death. Although she may enjoy the income from this trust during her life, it will not be taxed in her estate when she dies.

INTER VIVOS (LIVING) TRUSTS

Essential Features: In contrast to a testamentary trust which comes into existence when the grantor dies, **the living trust is created during the grantor's lifetime.** The provisions of the trust instrument include instructions for the management of the trust property, disposition of the income, length of time the trust is to last, and the ultimate disposition of the property to the named beneficiary(ies). The grantor can arrange for the trust income to be paid to himself or herself or can specify that it be paid to or accumulated for the beneficiary. The trust may be **revocable** (cancelable at the will of the grantor) or **irrevocable** (no right to cancel or change the provisions of the trust).

Purposes: There is a relationship between the **purpose** of the trust and the **kind** of trust used. When a **revocable trust** is established, the grantor usually is seeking relief (either from himself or for some other beneficiary) from custody, management, and investment of the trust property. **There are no tax advantages:** while the grantor lives, the trust income is taxed to the grantor; when that person dies, the property is taxed in **his or her estate.**

The **irrevocable trust** is in the gift category. It is a gift of immediate (or eventual) income and trust property. By naming one or more members of the family as beneficiary, the estate owner can reduce current income taxes and reduce administration expenses (for, of course, the trust property is excluded from the probate estate at death).

The **life insurance trust** is a special type of trust having many important uses and advantages. Perhaps the most common arrangement is the **personal life insurance trust** wherein the grantor designates the trustee as beneficiary of his or her life insurance. The trust instrument may give the trustee wide discretionary powers or may give specific instructions as to the payments of the proceeds. Generally, the purpose of such a trust is to obtain **greater flexibility of payments than the regular settlement options permit.** The trust may be **funded** (premiums paid from income provided by other property placed in the trust) or **unfunded** (premiums paid out of the grantor's pocket).

The **contingent life insurance trust** is a modification of the personal life insurance trust. Life insurance proceeds are arranged to be paid to a primary beneficiary under the policies' usual settlement options. **If the primary beneficiary dies after the insured but before receiving all payments due, then the unpaid balances of all policies flow into a contingent trust** set up for the purpose of distributing the remaining proceeds to contingent beneficiaries. If the primary beneficiary **predeceases** the insured, all proceeds are paid directly to the trust upon the insured's death. The contingent life insurance trust offers these big advantages:

a. **consolidation of miscellaneous proceeds into one centrally administered fund,**
b. **elimination of the bother and expense involved in providing a guardian of property for minors and**
c. **extreme flexibility in distributing proceeds in accordance with children's changing needs throughout the years.**

When a personal life insurance trust is **irrevocable and unfunded,** it provides flexibility of distribution AND some tax advantages. If the estate owner relinquishes all incidents of ownership in the life insurance policies placed in trust, **the proceeds are considered a gift and generally will not be included in the donor's estate at death.** However, if the incidents of ownership are transferred within three years of the donor's death, the proceeds would be brought back into the donor's estate under the estate tax rules of the 1976 Tax Reform Act. Also, if the donor's estate is the beneficiary of the policies, that, too, will bring the proceeds back into his estate.

Under this method, the owner of a large estate **can provide estate liquidity** by authorizing the trustee to lend money to or buy estate property from the executor, in an amount sufficient to meet settlement costs and taxes. In turn, the executor should be authorized in the estate owner's will to borrow from or sell property to the trustee.

OUTRIGHT INTER VIVOS (LIVING) GIFTS

The essentials and purposes of living gifts have been outlined previously. However, there is a special kind of living gift that deserves brief mention here. It is called an **inter vivos gift of limited property interest.** Through this device, an estate owner may give a certain beneficiary (usually a spouse) the privilege of using a piece of property and enjoying the income from it as long as that beneficiary lives. Upon the death of the first beneficiary, the property passes outright to one or more secondary beneficiaries. The first beneficiary is called a "life tenant" and the secondary beneficiaries are called "remaindermen." The right to use property and receive income from it is called a "life estate."

As an example of such a gift, a male estate owner transfers $50,000 of stock to his family, with his dependent mother entitled to all dividends for life and the stock going to his children at his mother's death. The dividends are a gift of present interest; the stock, a gift of future interest. The transfer results in a **savings in income taxes** (with dividends taxed in the mother's lower bracket). But gifts of future interest do not qualify for the $10,000 annual exclusion.

JOINTLY OWNED PROPERTY

Essential Features: Property may be placed in joint and survivorship title. This is a frequently used arrangement in estate planning, with property held on a husband-wife, joint ownership basis. It is common, for example, for an estate owner to place title to the home of a tenancy by the entirety with the spouse. Often, they will own a bank account with right of survivorship.

Purposes: Upon the death of one joint tenant, the **full title to the property rests in the survivor**

without the delay and expense of probate. In many states a tenancy by the entirety is not subject to inheritance tax. Property in joint ownership qualifies for the marital deduction but, of course, it is subject to federal estate tax when the survivor dies.

AGREEMENTS RELATING TO BUSINESS INTERESTS

Where estate owners have an interest in a business, they have available to them various forms of business agreements for the liquidation of their interests at death. The essential features and purposes of these agreements are fully described in the next chapter, "Business Insurance." Among other advantages, such agreements **eliminate shrinkage in values at death, assist in establishing proper federal estate tax valuation of business interests, and represent an ideal source of cash with which to settle the estate.**

OPPORTUNITIES FOR SERVICE IN ESTATE PROTECTION

We have examined briefly a number of estate planning devices. The process of assisting in the planning of a client's estate consists of bringing such arrangements into harmonious adjustment, in order to achieve the estate owner's objectives. Unfortunately, this problem of coordination is often neglected. Many people become so occupied with the building up of their estates that they give little consideration to plans of conservation and distribution which will most efficiently promote the future welfare of their heirs.

It is in this area that the well-informed life underwriter finds great opportunities for service. And, it is obvious that such valuable service will lead, naturally, to substantial sales of life insurance, the development of a **high-level clientele,** and the building of **centers of influence** who are indeed influential in the community.

But a final word of caution: The life underwriter must not invade the well-defined territories of the attorney, accountant or trust officer. He or she is "within bounds" in discussing with the client all matters pertaining to the estate and pointing out the legal, tax and accounting problems involved. However, the object should be (1) **to demonstrate to the client the compelling necessity of getting personal affairs in order,** (2) **to induce the client to consult with other professional advisers whose services are required** and, of course, (3) **to persuade the client to buy the amount of insurance that has been proven necessary for estate liquidity and family security.**

9

Business Insurance

Here are salient facts to prepare you for sole proprietor, key person, partnership or close corporation business insurance discussions. By keeping this with you constantly, you will never be at a loss for powerful business insurance sales points.

This section will be invaluable to help you get "in tune" for a business insurance interview, as a reference source in the actual interview, and as a helpful guide in preparing business insurance proposals.

A FERTILE FIELD

Big Market: Independent businesses have always been a staple in the American economy. At the height of the economic boom of the 1980s, new business starts arrived at a peak during 1986 to 1988 at about 66,000 per month, or more than 788,000 per year. Economic cycles naturally have their effect on growth figures but there is no question that an expanding business market offers great potential for the insurance agent.

An Easy-to-See Market: Business people are available during the course of the business day, and a professional approach in this market puts the insurance agent on a level with those of other salespersons.

Growing Market: Not only is the business community itself growing, but the list of products to sell has expanded enormously, i.e., pension plans, 401(k)s, health coverages and a substantial array of other protection and investment vehicles.

A Valuable Market:

- **Larger sales**—more of the 50's, 100's, 500's, 1,000,000's, etc.
- **Multiple sales**—often more than a one-life sale for a one-time effort.
- **Automatic repeat sales**—to increase protection on the same lives as the business grows.
- **Automatic new business**—to take care of added or replacement personnel.

- **Good persistency**—with easier-to-get business dollars going into annual premiums.
- **Centers of influence**—for other business cases and estate planning of well-paid executives.

YOUR RESPONSIBILITY

You, as a career underwriter and a financial planner, should have a clear understanding of the fundamental uses of business insurance. You should be in a position to recognize situations calling for the use of business insurance plans and be prepared to enumerate the specific advantages and the major points of such plans. The sale of business life insurance may be relatively uncomplicated at times, such as in the necessity for protection of business owner or stockholder heirs. More technical knowledge is needed for the sale and installation of worker benefit plans and special arrangements for highly compensated employees. While many details can be left to trust officers, attorneys and accountants, the salesperson needs to know many basic specifics about tax laws and particularly aspects of discrimination and fiscal compliance with the Internal Revenue Code, ERISA and Department of Labor regulations.

KEY-PERSON INSURANCE

The priceless asset of every successful business is not its plant—or equipment—or capital—or accounts receivable. These assets are valuable **only to the extent that people in management can utilize them profitably.**

The U.S. Department of Commerce says:

> "Almost every business has one or more people upon whom it depends heavily for its major success. Frequently it is the proprietor or manager. It might be the financial person, upon whose shoulders rests the firm's credit . . . it might be the sales manager . . . it might be a chemist, engineer or scientist whose efforts produce the firm's lifeblood of ideas."

This statement results from a Department of Commerce study of **570 business failures** in which the major bankruptcy causes were found to be:

1. Unwise management
2. Abuse and over-extension of credit
3. Adverse personal factors

It is obvious that the priceless asset of a business is not found in its property values—**but lies in its human life values, the brainpower and character of management.**

What Happens When a Key Person Dies

The death of a key person can result in a money loss more disastrous than any loss caused by fire, theft, flood or tornado! Here are some of the ruinous effects of a key person's death:

- **Losses through errors of judgment of less competent replacements.**
- **Losses through evaporation of goodwill.**
- **Losses in company's credit standing.**
- **Losses through competition that no longer can be met.**
- **Losses in hiring and training a new person.**
- **Losses through impaired morale of other workers.**

Business people accept without question the wisdom of protecting the company against the loss of its **property values.** They take care to insure the physical assets against losses from fire, windstorm, flood, etc. They take every precaution in insuring **capital assets** against embezzlement and theft. Yet protection against the loss of the **management assets of the business may be a far more vital need.** Moreover, the fire, theft, or flood may never occur—but death comes to every person, sooner or later.

How the Insurance Plan Works

The business

- determines the key person's profit-making value that would be lost at death.
- applies for insurance in this amount on the key person's life.
- pays the premiums.
- owns the policy.
- is the beneficiary of the policy.
- can borrow against the policy, surrender it for cash, retain all rights to it.

At the key person's death the business gets cash

- to stabilize the business and keep it running.
- to assure creditors that all is well.
- to assure customers that business will continue as usual.
- to retire pressing obligations.
- to continue paying salaries.
- to hire and train the successor.
- to pay a temporary monthly income to the key person's surviving spouse.
- to be used countless ways that may be advantageous in offsetting the loss of the key person.

And the cash comes to the business

- at once, when the need for it arises.

- free of federal income tax—**practically the only way a business today can receive tax-free income!**

Summary of Advantages of Key-Person Business Insurance

If the key person dies prematurely, the plan guarantees that: Cash will be available immediately to absorb the shock to the business. **Business credit** will be maintained. Money will be there to **hire and train a new person** and to offset smaller profits until the replacement is capable. **Confidence** on the part of customers, suppliers and employees **will remain intact.** The addition to surplus, coming from the life insurance payment, is a **tax-free increase.**

If the key person lives to retirement, the plan guarantees that: The **ever-growing cash value** will help tide the business over a stormy period. The policy will serve as **collateral for confidential loans** at a fair, guaranteed rate of interest. Extra funds will be available **for expansion.** Such funds are **secure against loss** and require **no investment worries.** Yearly increases in cash value are **not taxable. Morale** of all employees is strengthened. **Credit stand-**

ing of the business is enhanced. Values can be used to supplement the **key person's retirement plan.**

And the cost is so nominal: A surprisingly small investment—only the difference between the net premium paid and the increase in cash value for any year.

SOLE PROPRIETORSHIP INSURANCE

There are many advantages of the one-owner type of business, the most important of which are simplicity of organization and operation, and centralized control in the experienced hands of the owner. However, **these very advantages may turn into serious disadvantages** upon the death of the sole proprietor. Here are the problems that might arise:

Sole Proprietorship Problems

- The success of the business generally has depended on the skill, personality, reputation and management ability of the owner. **He or she is truly a key person, and when death comes these assets die also.**
- With the owner's human life values removed, the business is worth **only the liquidation value of**

stock, fixtures, equipment, plus accounts receivable that may be hard to collect. The surviving family can get only a fraction of the money the business was worth when the owner was alive.

- The owner's personal assets and business assets become one when the owner dies. Also, **business debts and personal debts become one and the same.** The estate becomes liable for all business obligations. This may force liquidation of valuable family assets in order to meet these obligations.
- A business that has been producing a good income for the family becomes, at the owner's death, a defunct business that **is no longer capable of producing anything** except what can be recovered through a forced sale.

Possible Solutions

If the family is to continue running the business: With substantial insurance on the owner's life to provide a special business continuation fund, there will be cash to absorb the shock to the business arising from the loss of the key person. Continuation of the business by the family may be the owner's choice, providing there are family members who have actual or potential management capabilities.

If the family is to liquidate the business: Sufficient insurance on the owner's life is needed to offset the difference between the going value of the business during his or her lifetime and the liquidation value of the business at the owner's death.

Thus, the family will receive the full value of the business—the liquidation value plus the insurance proceeds, which proceeds, incidentally, should be large enough to offset any remaining business obligations.

If key employees are to buy and continue the business: Selected key employees purchase insurance on the owner's life in a total amount equal to a fair price for the business. This is combined with an agreement whereby these employees agree to buy and the owner's estate agrees to sell the business at a certain price or at a price that can be determined from a procedure set forth in the agreement.

This type of business continuation plan, funded with life insurance, offers many advantages.

Advantages to the Proprietor of Selling to Association Under an Insurance Funded Agreement

- Provides a guaranteed market for the business at death.

- Transfers it to those most interested in its future, at a fair and prearranged price.
- Arranges for continuity of both management and personnel, a fact which will improve credit standing.
- Increases the interest of the employees in the future of the business, makes it a mutual endeavor, and provides a new incentive for employee cooperation.
- Builds general employee morale, because even those who are not included under the plan know that the business will not automatically collapse with the proprietor's death and that their jobs are stable and secure.
- Starts a reserve fund which may be used in purchasing the interest prior to death, if circumstances should make it desirable to retire from business activity.
- Makes loved ones independent of the future of the business, which the owner cannot manage after death. The death rate of businesses is notoriously high. No prudent person wishes to leave a family's fate to uncertain future conditions.

Only the life insurance plan will provide the cash to purchase the business upon the owner's

death. It provides exactly the right amount at exactly the time it is needed.

PARTNERSHIP BUSINESS INSURANCE

In order to sell partnership business insurance on a sound basis, the underwriter needs, first of all, a clear understanding of the effect of death on a business partnership. The death effect is the key to a powerful sales presentation.

What Does Death Do to a Partnership?

The death of a partner **automatically dissolves the partnership.**

! ! !

The surviving partner acts as a "liquidating trustee" for the purpose of **winding up the business**—unless there is a prearranged business continuation plan.

! ! !

After the business has been wound up (assuming there is no business continuation plan), **an accounting** must be made to the executor of the deceased partner's estate and the proceeds divided with the estate.

! ! !

During this process of business termination the business **cannot be operated** except to complete

> In the absence of express agreement to the contrary, every partnership is dissolved by the death of a partner.—*40 Am. Jur., Sec. 285*

existing contracts or to sell off merchandise for cash. If the surviving partner incurs any new obligations, he or she is personally liable.

! ! !

If the deceased partner was in debt to the company at the time of death, the estate will be required to **settle the account in cash.**

! ! !

The surviving partner has **no prior right to buy the deceased's interest** in the business. The surviving partner cannot take over the assets and goodwill of the partnership without the consent of the executor of the deceased's estate. He must convert everything into cash at the best price obtainable.

! ! !

In short, death of a partner destroys effectively, automatically and permanently the partnership as it existed prior to death.

What Choice Has a Surviving Partner?

When death comes to one member of a partnership the surviving partner faces **liquidation** or **reorganization** of the business. One or the other is inevitable.

Either the surviving partner or the deceased partner's heirs can choose to **liquidate. But neither can choose to reorganize the business without the consent of the other**—unless there has been a bona fide agreement set up prior to the death of any partner.

Now let's look at some of the results of **liquidation** or **reorganization.**

If liquidation is chosen:

- Surviving partners **sell themselves out of a job**. They have to start building a business all over again, or go to work for somebody else.

- The heirs will receive only what their share of the property assets will bring on the auction block. There will be **no future income—no guarantee of security**.

- Similarly, surviving partners get only their share of the receipts from the sale of business assets. They get **nothing** for the goodwill of the business, and **very little return** for their heavy investment of time, sweat and personal funds.

If reorganization is chosen the procedure is likely to be dictated by the heirs and must take one of the following forms:

- **Taking in the heirs as new business partners.** But if they are incompetent or inactive, the surviving partner does all the work, assumes all the responsibilities—and still divides the profits.

- **Accepting as a new partner the person to whom the heirs sell their business interest.** But the buyer may be unacceptable or lacking in ability. The new partner may even be a competitor who wants to exert a control over the business.

- **Selling the surviving partner's interest to the heirs.** But it may take a long time to agree on the price, and payment may have to be delayed until the deceased's estate is settled. Meanwhile, the business deteriorates and the surviving partner is out of work.

- **Purchasing of the heirs' interest by the surviving partner.** But the heirs may hold out for an unreasonable price. Even if the price can be agreed upon, raising the money may be a difficult or impossible hurdle for the surviving partner.

Obviously, what is needed is a prearranged buy-sell agreement (as described on the following pages), **properly funded with life insurance.**

The Insurance Funded Buy-Sell Agreement

Since no two partnerships are exactly alike, there is no standard form of agreement. The provisions of each contract must be individually "fitted" by the attorney to the circumstances. The points generally covered are:

1. **Parties to the Agreement**: all partners and the selected trustee, if any.
2. **Purpose of the Agreement**: to clarify the intention of the parties.
3. **"First Offer" Commitment**: a requirement that any partner who wishes to sell his or her interest must first offer it to the other partners at the purchase price that would be effective at the death of the partner who desires to sell.
4. **Commitment to Sell and to Buy**: each partner agrees to **sell** (at death) his or her interest to the surviving partners; surviving partners agree to **buy** the deceased partner's interest.
5. **Price to Be Paid**: either a set price or a clear valuation formula or price-fixing procedure.

6. **Life Insurance Financing**: explanation of how life insurance is being used to fund the agreement.
7. **Schedule of Policies**: identification and description of life insurance policies.
8. **Provision for Adding, Substituting or Withdrawing Policies**: to take into account changes in the value of the business.
9. **Adjustment for Difference Between Purchase Price and Insurance Proceeds**: the disposition to be made of extra proceeds, if any, or method of paying any balance due.
10. **Payment of Premiums**: how paid among partners.
11. **Ownership of Policies and Restrictions on Use**: ownership rights and exercise of rights in keeping with the terms of the agreement.
12. **Beneficiary Arrangements**: specifying to whom proceeds are to be paid.
13. **Disposition of Insurance on Lives of Surviving Partners**: right of survivors to purchase own policies from deceased's estate for a reasonable sum.
14. **Creditor Protection for Deceased's Estate**: with survivors assuming all obligations of the partnership.

15. **Provision for Amending, Revoking or Terminating the Agreement:** by joint action as circumstances warrant.

A Common Objection

Frequently, you will find that members in a partnership have had the foresight to draw up a valid buy-sell agreement. **But they have not taken the logical step of arranging for life insurance to make sure the funds will be available to carry out the agreement.** Too often, they object to the purchase of life insurance on the grounds that it is not necessary. They do not anticipate any difficulty in securing the necessary money to purchase a deceased's interest. **It is sound sales procedure to point out the probable difficulties.**

Why Life Insurance?

A partnership buy-sell agreement **is only as good as the financial agreement that has been made to support it.** Without the help of life insurance, where can the surviving partner get the cash?

From personal assets?

In most cases, **the partners' personal assets are tied up in the firm,** for profits are often plowed back into the business to insure stability and promote expansion. If personal funds are available, the survivor has to pay **100 cents on the dollar** for the deceased's business interest.

From the firm's assets?

Ordinarily, the attempt to dispose of firm assets (largely found in inventory, equipment, real estate and other nonliquid items) results in **tremendous losses**.

From the firm's profits, over a period of time?

But **profits are likely to dwindle** after the loss of a partner's efforts and ability. Probably **someone will have to be hired** to take the deceased partner's place—another drain on profits. If the surviving partners increase their own income, they also increase their taxes appreciably. And if they pay off the debt on the installment plan, they pay 100 cents on the dollar, plus interest.

By borrowing the money?

But death of a partner **wrecks the credit of the firm**. The defunct business can't borrow, and the future of a reorganized business is **too uncertain** to warrant a lender's taking the risk. And even if money could be borrowed, it must be repaid with 100-cent dollars—plus interest.

HOW THE PLAN WORKS

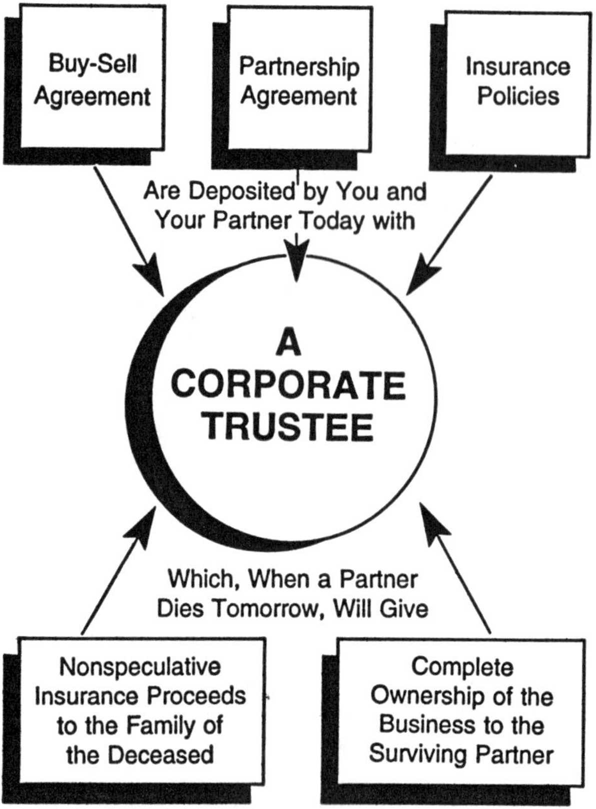

By setting up a sinking fund?

It would **take years** to create an adequate fund while the need for it might arise at any moment. And **why tie up large sums of money** that could be used much more profitably in the business?

Yes, Life Insurance! Because—

- **It delivers** the purchase price the moment it is needed!
- **It provides** cash on the line, in full payment!
- **It converts** the heirs' uncertain interest into guaranteed dollars!
- **It gives** the business to the surviving partner, free and clear!
- **It eliminates** the need for tying up business capital!
- **It is purchased** with discounted dollars, for premiums seldom equal proceeds!
- **It provides** cash and loan values for use in business emergencies!

IT IS THE ONLY SURE AND SENSIBLE WAY!

CLOSE CORPORATION INSURANCE

Close corporation or stock retirement insurance represents one of the major business life insurance markets of today. It is **peculiarly suited** to the needs of the thousands upon thousands of **small and medium-size businesses** of the country, where the stock control is held in limited hands. To impress such stockholders with the need of stock retirement insurance, it is **essential to give them a clear picture of the effect of the death** of a key stockholder on the interests of the business and other stockholders.

When a Stockholder Dies, What Is the Situation?

The problems involved at the death of a stockholder must be considered in the light of (a) the effect on the heirs of the deceased and (b) the effect on the survivors. Both sides must be presented with equal force since no one can tell which of the stockholders may die first. In the eyes of the law, a corporation lives on, unaffected by the death of any individual stockholder.

Actually, however, while the death of a business associate may leave the corporation's **legal** structure intact, it can never leave the corporation's **personal** structure intact. On the surface, the same company under the same name is conducting its business in the same old way. **But the same people are not running its affairs.** The deceased stockholder's interest lives on intact after death, but it is no longer that individual's interest. Behind the deceased stockholder's interest stands an administrator or an executor, and the family and the heirs of the deceased. A **living interest has automatically become the interest of an estate. And the viewpoints of the two interests are fundamentally opposed.**

The living interest, as represented by the surviving stockholders, thinks in terms of management and capital, in terms of plant expansion, of long-term merchandising programs, of profits used to increase production and to step up sales and distribution. The living interest derives its profits largely from salary allowances for work done, and hence views dividends as of secondary importance.

The estate interest, as represented by the executor or administrator and the family of the deceased associate, is concerned almost exclusively with the need and desire for **present income,** for it ordinarily shares in the corporation profits only insofar as those profits are distributed as dividends. As a result, the estate interest views dividends, rather than the building up of adequate expansion and emergency reserves, as of primary importance.

Without a Funded Buy-Sell Agreement

The surviving stockholders must:

- Accept the estate and heirs as new stockholders in the business, giving them all the rights they are entitled to under the law, and sharing profits with them even though they are inactive or incompetent—**or**
- Run the chance that the deceased stockholder's shares will be put up for sale to the highest bidder, perhaps a competitor—**or**
- Accept as a business associate anyone who buys the deceased's share, even though the person is unwanted, unliked or incapable—**or**
- Haggle with an uncompromising lawyer or judge of a probate court as to the value of the deceased's interest—**or**
- Sell out and lose what they have been building up for years.

The heirs of the deceased must:

- Offer their shares to the highest bidder, and be satisfied with the low price that a **desperation sale** usually brings—**or**
- Assume control of the business (if majority stockholders) **even though** they may not know anything about, or care anything about, the business—**or**

- Retain a "nuisance interest" in the business (if minority stockholders), without a significant voice in management and getting **only a meager income** from dividends—or **no income at all,** if management decides to retain earnings for business expansion—**or**
- Just hold on and take the chance that the shares may increase in value, even though the chances are that the value **will decrease** as the result of the shock to the business of an owner's death.

In Preparing for the Close Corporation Interview

1. Before you go into the interview, find out who controls the majority of the stock, so you will know who has most at stake.
2. Find out in advance, if possible, who dominates the business affairs of the corporation, so that your appeal may be directed to the individual or individuals in a position to say "yes" or "no" to your proposal.
3. Know as much as possible about the families of those most interested so that you can use the "family angle" in making your most effective points.

4. Be sure to place emphasis upon the benefits of an **insured** business continuation plan to all parties concerned, for each stockholder will want assurance that, live or die, his or her interests will be equally well protected. The outline of benefits on the following pages will be helpful.

Advantages of the Buy-Sell Agreement—TO THE SURVIVING STOCKHOLDERS

Advantages inherent in the agreement itself, assuming adequate financing:

- **It prevents** the dangers and the frustrations of having to go into business with the widow or children or executor of the deceased stockholder.

- **It removes** any possibility of unwelcome outsiders obtaining a control in the business.

- **It permits** important business decisions to be made, without explanations to persons unfamiliar with the business, or to persons whose interests are opposed to the business.

- **It averts** any interruptions of business momentum, so that creditors and employees do not become worried about the future of the corporation.

- **It keeps** control of the business in experienced hands and enables management to operate **unhampered,** at a time when freedom of action is vital to the continuation of the business.
- **It allows** the associates to set the sales price of their stockholdings, in a friendly spirit of mutual consideration, rather than have the price influenced by an outsider who is unfamiliar with the factors involved or unsympathetic with the business.

Extra advantages to surviving stockholders when life insurance is used to support the buy-sell agreement:

- •• **It provides** the money necessary to retire the stockholdings of a deceased associate—**immediately**—exactly when the money is needed.
- •• **It prevents** a weakening of the business which would result from draining off cash or selling nonliquid assets.
- •• **It eliminates** the need for borrowing and being in debt for years. Consider how much the corporation would have to earn **before taxes** to pay off the principal and the interest on it.
- •• **It guarantees** the principal for a yearly deposit of only about one-half the normal interest rate on

the principal, instead of requiring a payoff of principal **plus** interest.

- •• **It frees** substantial money for use in the business—money that otherwise might have to be tied up in a sinking fund.
- •• **It brings** an enormous appreciation if a stockholder dies within five or ten years. And if the associates live for many years, the yearly net charge for the insurance (premiums less cash value) will be relatively small.
- •• **It creates** extra borrowing power for expansion or business emergencies.

Advantages of the Buy-Sell Agreement—TO THE HEIRS OF THE DECEASED

Advantages inherent in the agreement itself, assuming adequate financing:

- **It guarantees** to the heirs that they will receive a fair price for the deceased's stockholdings, a price which was agreed to by the deceased, himself, before his death.
- **It makes it** unnecessary for the heirs to become participants in the business and dependent on the uncertainty of dividend income.

- **It wipes out** the possibility of friction between the heirs and surviving business owners.

- **It provides** a guaranteed market for the deceased's shares, at a stipulated price, thus no one is going to "drive a hard bargain" with the heirs.

- **It prevents** the heirs from suffering the embarrassment of pleading with the surviving associates for "a little money to get along on."

- **It sets the value** of the deceased's shares for estate tax purposes, thus preventing estate taxes from being appreciably inflated due to the unusually high appraisals of such business interests.

Extra advantages to the heirs, when life insurance is used to finance the buy-sell agreement:

•• **It guarantees** that the heirs will receive CASH, rather than stock, the value of which may drop alarmingly, or promissory notes that may or may not be paid eventually.

•• **It provides** the cash at once—when it is needed most to offset the sudden loss of the deceased stockholder's income.

•• **It gives** the estate, the heirs, and most important, the widow or widower, a maximum return on the stockholdings, since it avoids expensive legal actions and technical delays.

- •• **It prevents** any loss to the heirs in case business suffers because of depressions, business reverses, mismanagement or even bankruptcy.
- •• **It makes it unnecessary** for the heirs to rely on whatever form of collateral the surviving associates may be able to scrape together.
- •• **It offers** security that can be counted on with absolute certainty. So the heirs, and particularly the widow or widower, can have the advantage of an overall plan of family protection into which the proceeds of the business interest have been included as an important part.

Insurance Funded Buy-Sell Agreement

Individual cases vary to such an extent that no "standard" form can be illustrated. In the attorney's drafting of the tailor-made agreement, the following provisions are generally included:

1. **Parties to the Agreement**: Ordinarily all stockholders, together with the trustee, if any, selected by them.
2. **Purpose of the Agreement:** The purpose and intent of the parties to the agreement.
3. **"First Offer" Commitment:** Agreement of each stockholder not to sell stock without first

offering it for sale to other stockholders at the price that would be effective at his or her death.

4. **Commitment to Sell and Buy:** Each stockholder agrees that his or her stock be sold, at his or her death, to surviving stockholders; surviving stockholders agree to buy deceased stockholder's shares.
5. **Valuation Method** Either an exact purchase price of shares fixed in advance, or a clear-cut formula to be applied at death.
6. **Identification of Stock Certificates:** Provision of identifying stock certificates as being subject to the agreement.
7. **Financing with Life Insurance:** Explanation of use of life insurance to fund the agreement and recording of policies.
8. **Provision for Adding, Subtracting or Withdrawing Policies:** In line with future changes in value of the stock.
9. **Adjustment for Difference Between Purchase Price and Insurance Proceeds:** The disposition of extra proceeds, if any, or method of paying any balance due.
10. **Payment of Premiums:** How they are to be paid and by whom.
11. **Ownership of Policies and Restrictions on Use:** Ownership rights and exercise of rights in line with terms of agreement.

12. **Beneficiary Arrangements:** The proper and logical person to receive proceeds.
13. **Disposition of Policies on Lives of Surviving Stockholders:** Method of purchase from deceased's estate.
14. **Provision for Amending, Revoking or Terminating Agreement:** By joint action as circumstances may warrant.

Without Life Insurance

If the buy-sell agreement is not supported by life insurance that automatically provides cash to buy out the heirs, then in order to purchase the stock of the deceased, the surviving stockholders must:

- **Seek a bank loan** or other loan at the very time the **future of the business is most in doubt** and credit hardest to obtain—**or**

- **Raid the assets of the firm** right at the time cash needs are greatest, when the business is going through a period of readjustment, **when every dollar is needed** to offset the shock caused by the death of an active associate—**or**

- **Pay off the heirs over a period of years,** which adds up to a staggering price when you consider

HOW BUSINESS INSURANCE SOLVES THE PROBLEM

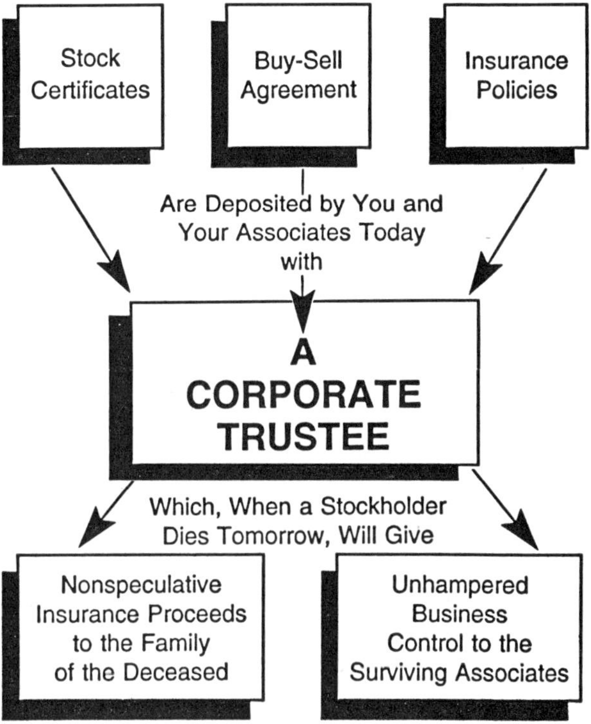

how much the corporation **has to earn before taxes** to write off the principal **plus** interest—**or**

- **Pour their personal assets into the business** and jeopardize their own and their families' security—the very thing they incorporated to avoid! Look at the problems . . . what a situation!

NOW LOOK AT THE LIFE INSURANCE PLAN . . . WHAT A CONTRAST!!

Approach Questions

The use of thought-provoking questions is an effective approach to the discussion of the stock purchase insurance plan. For example, you might begin your questioning in this way:

Mr. (or Ms.) Prospect, suppose the telephone should ring just now and you were informed that one of your major stockholding associates had met with a fatal automobile accident. Having set the stage, you could follow up with a series of disturbing questions such as these:

- Would you want to buy the deceased's interest in the firm?
- Have you the ready cash to make such a purchase?
- Would you want the widow or widower in the business as an active stockholder?

- For example, would you want to take someone else into the firm in place of the widow or widower, without the right to approve the new person?
- Even with your approval, how long would it take you to find the right person?
- Could the individual you'd select finance the purchase of the deceased's shares of stock?
- Suppose you wanted to buy it instead of taking anybody else in, how big a check would you have to write?
- If you can't sign a check of that size, how would you like an insurance company to sign it?

A HEAVY PRICE

Borrowing to pay off a partnership interest or close corporation stock purchase at the death of a partner or stockholder **is expensive**!

THE LOGIC OF BUSINESS LIFE INSURANCE

Only two forms of business values: Dollars at work—invested capital. **People at work**—invested capacity.

AMORTIZING $100,000 OVER TEN YEARS AT 6.75% INTEREST

Year	*Principal*	*Interest*	*Total Payments**
1	$ 7,250.48	$6,528.41	$13,779
2	7,755.31	6,023.57	"
3	8,295.30	5,483.59	"
4	8,872.88	4,906.01	"
5	9,490.68	4,288.20	"
6	10,151.50	3,627.39	"
7	10,858.33	2,920.56	"
8	11,614.37	2,164.52	"
9	12,423.06	1,355.83	"
10	13,288.05	490.84	"
Becomes	$100,000		$137,790

*The above calculation is based on a monthly repayment figure of $1,148.24—amounts have been rounded off to the nearest dollar figure.

Ten Long Years of Debt!

A Total of $137,790 Needed to Pay for the $100,000 Business Interest!

$37,790 of Interest on a $100,000 Business Purchase Obligation!

Contrast this to the swift, certain, taxless and debtless way in which the Business Life Insurance Plan operates!

Either value is destructible: **Loss of invested capital** would mean a shrinkage in profits. **Loss of invested capacity** usually results in a much greater shrinkage in profits—and a shrinkage in the value of invested capital.

Property values are always protected: It is just good business to **insure property values** against loss through fire, storm, theft and such hazards.

But there is a greater hazard: Loss of human capacity **through death** is a total and much more devastating loss than any of the losses against which property values are protected.

Offsetting this hazard is imperative: Business life insurance meets this danger by pouring into the business the **cash value of the human capacity that death has destroyed**. Thus the net position, with respect to profit-earning ability and business values, is unchanged.

Protects living interests of the business: Every officer, proprietor, partner, or stockholder of a business is deeply concerned about the **continuity** of the organization. To each of them, it means his or her job, income, family welfare and the amount of return on and the future value of the investment in the business.

While the owners live, business life insurance **stabilizes the capital structure of the firm and reinforces its credit standing.** It is an effective shock absorber to help the business ride smoothly over the financial bumps and ruts that all organizations encounter at some time or other.

Strengthens family interests: In event an owner dies, the business insurance plan **turns business holdings into liquid assets**. The family gets 100 percent of the deceased's business interest—at once—in cash.

Through business life insurance, **the future uncertainty of the business** is converted for the family into the certainty of **cash**—guaranteed by contract.

Makes both interests secure: Business insurance provides **continuity of profits and business values** if the owner lives and **a guaranteed market and a fair price** for the owner's interest at death.

BUSINESS INSURANCE QUOTES

Do you carry a **key-person depreciation account**?

" "

Key-person insurance dollars are tax-free dollars. **How else** could your business enjoy tax-free income?

" "

Are you willing to have **your partner's widow or widower** do the work your partner is doing?

" "

Is your business for sale? Will it be for sale after your death? **How do you know,** if you won't be here?

" "

If your partner had died **last night,** would you be open for business **today**?

" "

Any partnership that operates without a proper buy-sell agreement **is living on borrowed time.**

" "

Your business supports the family today. If you were to die, **would it go on supporting them**?

If you had made one down payment on your business associate's interest, and he or she died wouldn't you like knowing that **you would never be called on to pay the balance**—that the share would belong to you free and clear?

" "

Dividing a business between heirs and survivors is like **killing the goose that laid the golden egg.**

GROUP LIFE, HEALTH AND TAX-DEFERRED INVESTMENT AND RETIREMENT PLANS

Today's social and economic tides indicate that it is to the advantage of employers to take a keen interest in the financial programs of their management and worker associates. This employer awareness has resulted in a marked expansion of various plans sold on an employer basis.

The employee who knows that he or she is accumulating financial resources in the form of tax-deferred insurance or annuity contracts, 401(k) programs, SEPs and similar programs, feels less restless and insecure, does better work, has higher morale and generally has more of a feeling of loyalty to the employer. This employee is a much better influence among associates than the person who faces the constant fear that he or she, or loved ones, will meet financial problems with which they cannot cope.

Selling the Employee

Where the employee pays the entire cost, the sales points to emphasize are: (1) the plan gives an opportunity to secure the same type of plan ordinarily available only to the person able to pay a much larger monthly premium, (2) there is little danger of the policy's lapsing since premiums are paid automatically through payroll deductions and (3) the plan offers a painless cash accumulation plan.

Where the employee pays only part of the premium, **emphasize the return for his or her part of the premium**, showing how much the employer's contributions build up for the employee. Use all of your standard sales appeals for the placing of the contract. **Fit the plan into the insurance he or she owns and integrate it with Social Security benefits** to show what the whole program does.

Where tax deferral is a factor, emphasize how the tax deferral contributes to the end result by showing a larger accumulation for less money invested.

Selling To the Employer

To the employer, the advantages of a sound employee insurance or pension plan are manifold. The plan should be presented on a straight, good business basis. Major advantages are:

1. **The plan reduces** employee turnover because most employees do not want to lose benefits for themselves or their families.

2. **The plan enables** an employer to retire employees who are too old to meet the demands of their jobs, yet must be kept on the payroll as a matter of kindness and charity.
3. **The plan, properly explained** at the time of employment, enables a business to secure a better type of employee.
4. **The plan makes** for better work, because it reduces greatly the worry and unrest existing in the employee's mind when he or she feels financially insecure.
5. **The plan creates** added markets for the products of industry since the employee, because of the backlog of financial strength given by the plan, feels more free to spend normally.
6. **The plan is evidence** of the recognition of the modern management concept that depreciation of human life values must be provided for exactly as depreciation funds for plant and equipment are set up.

With the **tax deductions** offered by the government for employer contributions to qualified pension and profit-sharing plans, the employer can effect **large tax savings.**

Pensions

The pension area still represents a significant market for the life insurance agent even though restrictive legislation of the past few years has complicated employee benefit compliance and reporting requirements. Following are some basic characteristics of a few typical qualified plans.

Defined benefit pension: A plan based on a formula for a retirement fund paid according to the employee's length of service and annual earnings. Up to $200,000 of annual compensation (indexed for inflation) is allowed to be factored in for calculating retirement pay.

Defined contribution pension: The employer contributes annually a set amount for each year of the employee's participation in the plan. There is a maximum limit of $30,000 annually for such contributions. This type of arrangement is also known as a money purchase plan.

Target benefit plan: A combination of the above two wherein the formula benefit promised can be increased by reflecting investment earnings of the plan, or having a cost-of-living factor included.

Profit-sharing plan: A plan providing for generally a lump sum final payment at retirement or employee termination, using a formula based on annual profits. Recent legislation has determined that the employer does not necessarily have to have a profit in order to make a contribution, which makes the plan similar to a defined contribution plan.

401(k) plan: An adjunct to a profit-sharing plan that permits employees to defer taxes on part of their compensation deposited into the plan, up to $7,000 annually (adjusted for inflation). Employers may match these savings, either in cash or company stock.

ESOP: Acronym for Employee Stock Ownership Plan, a type of stock bonus defined contribution plan which invests primarily in securities of the employer. ESOPs are subject to the same general qualifications as a profit-sharing plan.

General Distribution Rules for Qualified Plans

Under provisions of Section 401(a)(14) of the Internal Revenue Code, qualified plans are mandated to provide for distributions not later than the participant's age 65, 10 years after the employee's entry into the plan and termination of service. While payments may be delayed at the employee's option, funds must begin a payout not later than April 1 in the year after the participant attains age 70½. Distribution can be in a lump sum or on a periodic payment schedule. There is a penalty of 50 percent imposed on delayed distributions that do not meet these restrictions. The tax is calculated on the difference between the amount that should have been distributed and the actual payment of funds.

These tax-deferred funds may be "rolled over" to another retirement plan, or to an IRA to continue their tax-sheltered provisions, subject, of course, to the above stipulations. For those individuals choosing a lump sum distribution, special one-time income averaging factors are available. The tax payable is basically determined as if it were on income received spread over a five-year period; however it is a special calculation with some other qualifying factors involved. In addition, the averaging can be elected only after age 59½. Previous to 1986, ten year averaging was allowed, and is still an option for retirees who were at least age 50 at that time. Capital gain treatment, still available for pre-1974 accumulations, may also be used, whichever method results in the least amount of tax. (The detailed computation is provided on IRS form 4972.) There is an additional excess distribution tax of 15 percent for payments which exceed $112,500 annually (adjusted for inflation) payable in addition to the regular income tax.

Cafeteria Plans

Cafeteria Plans, known also as Section 125 plans, are a type of flexible benefit health plan that is widely popular. The cafeteria plan is a written, legally enforceable plan separate from other company plans.

The major advantage of the cafeteria plan is as an adjunct to the basic medical reimbursement plan already in place. The base plan is usually paid for by the employer with some cost participation by the employee. This cost is paid by the employee with after-tax dollars. With the addition of the cafeteria plan, the employee is able to devise a personal plan from a wide list of benefits including reduced deductibles, higher maximum benefits, dependent coverage, additional group life insurance, vision and dental care and prescription drugs. Depending upon the type of plan, each optional benefit carries a price tag stated in terms of credits. Credits not used may be paid out in cash to the employee or used for other selected benefits. The employee also shares in the cost of the cafeteria plan, but payment is made with before-tax dollars, thus providing leverage to the participant.

Once the plan is put into effect, each employee decides the amount of funds to be set aside for each chosen benefit. If that benefit is not used up by the end of the plan year, the money in the fund, by IRS regulation, reverts to the employer, who may use the funds to offset regular benefit costs. Discrepancies like this can be avoided by a year-end adjustment by the employee, either changing the allocation of funding or the amount of salary reduction, if the plan permits.

A variation of cafeteria plans are Salary Reduction Flexible Spending Accounts (FSAs). The essence of this plan is in employee participants voluntarily electing to reduce compensation they would normally receive, and having these funds set aside to reimburse medical expenses. This is exactly the process followed in a 401(k) plan, except that the monies are not set aside for retirement, but are paid out on an annual basis. In addition to health benefits, these plans may offer such items as legal expense coverage, extra vacation days and educational expenses.

10

Retirement

In the area of retirement planning, many developments springing from federal legislation in recent years have special significance for life insurance agents and many of their prospects.

The enactment of the Employee Retirement Act of 1974 (ERISA), the Economic Recovery Act of 1981 (ERTA), and Tax Equity and Fiscal Responsibility Act of 1982 (TEFRA) increased the sales potential for many tax-deferred employee benefit plans. In more recent years, however, restrictions such as those incorporated in the Tax Reform Act of 1986, have curtailed some benefits. The following section describes in part some of the many opportunities that still exist for sales in this area of specialization.

KEOGH PLANS FOR THE SELF-EMPLOYED

The Self Employed Retirement Act of 1962 ushered in the tax-deferred vehicle known as the Keogh or HR-10 plan. The plan was designed to offer self-employed individuals a benefit equivalent to the pension provisions for corporate employees. Later legislation liberalized the provisions of the plan, and more recent tax reform brought Keogh plans into line with most corporate pension plan regulations. Two main differences that remain exclusive with Keogh plans are (1) Keogh plan loans to owner-employees are restricted while corporate plan loans are allowed and (2) contributions or benefits on behalf of self-employed individuals are based on net earnings, rather than on salary.

As a retirement plan for an unincorporated business, Keogh plans are suitable for sole proprietorships such as those of doctors, architects, accountants, writers and others, with or without employees. Under current regulations, the annual fully deductible contribution is limited to 25 percent of earned income up to a maximum of $30,000. Use of a defined benefit plan allows funding of an annual retirement benefit of $90,000 (as indexed for inflation). As is the case with corporate plans of this type, funds cannot be withdrawn minus a penalty until age 59½ and distributions must commence at age 70½. A 50 percent penalty applies (based on the difference between the amount that should have been distributed and the actual amount distributed) when distributions are not made.

Present law permits a self-employed person to set aside a certain portion of his or her earned income each year and deduct the entire amount from taxable income. Allowable deductible amounts are the lesser of 25 percent of compensation or $30,000. The use of a defined benefit plan can permit the funding of a benefit that does not exceed the lesser of 100 percent of employee annual compensation or $90,000 annually beginning at age 65, adjusted for inflation.

Participants in a Keogh plan are not taxed on such contributions made for their benefit, or on the income earned by the funds during the accumulation period. They are, of course, taxed on distributions made to them from the fund after retirement.

The amounts set aside in a Keogh plan cannot be withdrawn, except with a penalty, until age 59½. Withdrawals must commence before age 70.

ADVANTAGES OF AN INSURED KEOGH PLAN

Qualified Keogh plans may be funded by various means and in various ways. Self-employed individuals may invest their Keogh funds in certain life insurance contracts, variable annuity contracts, mutual funds, government bonds or a combination of these funding media. Certain plans call for the establishment of a trust or custodial account with a bank. Insurance companies also offer custodial type accounts.

A Keogh plan that is funded in whole or in part by life insurance products, including annuities, provides the safety of principal that is guaranteed by such contracts. Also, cash value insurance or annuity contracts can guarantee that retirement income will be paid as long as the insured or annuitant lives. Still another advantage of an insured plan is that it can guarantee substantially greater death benefits to the insured's survivors if the insured doesn't live to retire. And the pure insurance proceeds in such a plan are received by the beneficiary free of income tax.

Distributions from a tax-sheltered Keogh (HR-10) retirement plan will be subject to income tax, but after retirement, the tax obligations generally are much less than before.

INDIVIDUAL RETIREMENT ACCOUNTS

Individual Retirement Accounts (IRAs) have long been a staple for American investors of a wide variety of financial means to invest up to $2,000 per year and have their account earnings tax deferred. Prior to

1982, only persons not covered by qualified benefit plans were IRA eligible. From 1982 to 1986, most Americans, regardless of participation in other tax deferrals, could participate and have their contributions fully deductible. The Tax Reform Act of 1986 still allowed any income earner to open an IRA, but severely restricted deductibility. There may be future changes, since the plans are extremely popular. Since the enabling legislation of 1974, Americans have put more than $200 billion into IRAs. In the last year before deductibility was restricted, annual IRA deposits totalled almost $38 billion, representing almost one-third of all of the country's personal savings. Eighty percent of account funds deposited between 1982 and 1986 came from new savings and nearly two-thirds of IRA contributors came from middle- or lower-income households.

Under tax reform, the $2,000 annual contribution is still allowable. However, deductibility is limited for individuals who participate as employees in tax-deferral benefit plans. A full deduction is allowed for those earning $25,000 or less annually ($40,000 on a joint return), with a percentage deduction available for the next $10,000 in earnings, which is phased out completely above such levels. A major advantage still available for IRA accounts is the ability to receive rollover deposits from pension and profit-sharing funds in order to continue deferrals of taxes.

Who Is Eligible

Any wage earner under age 70½ is eligible to set up an IRA, whether self-employed or working for an employer. "Spousal" accounts may be established for non-working spouses for an additional $250. Income tax is payable when withdrawals are made from the account. Distributions may not occur without penalty before the account owner's age 59½. The penalty is 10 percent, levied on the amount drawn, and is payable in addition to the normal income tax. Exceptions to the penalty are made in the event of disability, correcting a previous excess contribution, or if disbursements are made according to a series of substantially equal periodic payments in connection with life expectancy calculations. Distributions from the account must commence the year following the account owner's attaining of age 70½.

Funding of IRAs

There are a variety of ways in which to invest IRA funds. Life insurance is no longer one of them. However, annuities are an allowable investment, along with a variety of other vehicles. Many financial institutions offer "self-directed" plans, which typically provide a limited pre-selected group of choices, often including a family of mutual funds. Actually, however, there is a wide range of possibilities, including common stocks and other securities, real property, limited partnerships and precious metals. Many trustees, however, will not offer such a variety of options.

SIMPLIFIED EMPLOYEE PENSIONS (SEPS)

Virtually any business can set up a Simplified Employee Pension Plan (SEP). The concept is basically a group IRA plan, and gives the agent the opportunity to offer an employer a pension plan that is practically maintenance-free and lacks the complication of government filing. There are no plan documents to update and the SEP may even be described as a no-cost 401(k) plan, because of the employee's ability to add voluntary deductible contributions.

A simple way to understand SEPs is to examine IRS form 5305-SEP. It contains complete explanations of SEP rules in question and answer form, and it serves as the actual official plan document. All that is necessary to adopt the plan is to enter the name of the business, answer several questions, check off a few boxes and have the form signed and dated.

A SEP allows an employer to contribute up to 15 percent of salary, counting compensation up to $200,000 (adjusted for inflation), with a ceiling of $30,000. The employee may add an additional contribution of $2,000 annually, up to $30,000. SARSEPs are salary reduction plans for businesses with 25 employees or less, wherein the employee can defer part of compensation. These plans may be installed as additions to the employer SEP, or they may stand alone. Employee instituted deferrals are limited to $7,000 annually (adjusted for inflation) and are based on 25 percent of compensation. All employee funds for SEPs, whether contributed by the employer or employee are immediately vested. Another convenience with SEP plans is that while other qualified plans must be finalized and adopted before the end of a fiscal year, the SEP allows more flexibility since that implementation need not occur until the due date of the employer's income tax return for the previous year.

LONG-TERM CARE

While many senior citizens have seen to it that they are provided with hospitalization insurance, the issue of long-term care coverage has come to the forefront in recent years. While insurers have achieved a great deal of progress in the first few policy generations, it is generally agreed that policy benefits need more refining. There is a confusing array of plans on the market. However, planners should ascertain that the contracts they recommend offer an adequate selection of benefits expressed in clear and readable terms. The better contracts will reference some of the following provisions:

1. Alzheimer's Disease—policy should cover this illness based on physician's diagnosis, rather than on any demonstrable sign; many contracts will not cover mental illness that has no organic basis.
2. Previous hospital stay—some contracts require a period of hospital stay before benefits can be paid; this is not a desirable feature.
3. Generation of benefits—advantageous contracts will pay benefits if insured cannot perform two or three daily living activities, such as eating, bathing, walking, dressing or standing, or if they cannot remember to perform them.
4. Home-care coverage—important benefit not always provided; many individuals will avoid institutions at all costs even though care is needed.
5. Guaranteed renewability—a highly recommended and important feature.

11

Some Sales Ideas

Here are some sales ideas for plans that have been popular in the life insurance market:

- Deferred Compensation
- Split-Dollar Plans
- Death Benefit Only (DBO)
- Group Long-Term Disability
- Pension Maximization

Each plan is relatively simple—easy to present—and the market is getting bigger and better all the time.

Ideas like these are selling millions of dollars of life insurance. Get your share!

DEFERRED COMPENSATION

There is a large market for deferred compensation plans. The selling of life insurance in relation to these plans is not a complex procedure, and the principles can be mastered readily by any capable life agent, without intensive, specialized study. Here is a field in which you can perform a valuable service to employers and their key personnel—and be extremely well paid for your efforts.

What Does a Deferred Compensation Plan Do? The purposes arise from two problems: (1) **High income taxes** make it almost impossible for highly paid executives to set aside an adequate portion of their net earnings for retirement; and (2) **the shortage of executive material** makes it difficult for employees to **attract and keep key people.** Thus, deferred compensation plans are designed to (1) **supplement pension plans for top executives or, if no pension plan exists, provide substantial retirement benefits exclusively for key personnel;** and (2) **enable the employer to attract high-caliber executives and assure their continued services.** Deferred compensation plans are ideal for accomplishing these purposes because the benefits can be achieved through long-run savings to the company and increased net income to the key employee.

How does deferred compensation work? It is a flexible plan, so there are many varieties. But most plans follow this general pattern:

1. A key executive is in such a high salary bracket **that further salary raises will largely be drained off in increased taxes.**
2. Instead of giving any additional salary, the company contracts to make a **fixed number of payments to the employee beginning at retirement,** when his or her increased exemptions and lower tax bracket will result in a greater net return.
3. Usually, but not necessarily, the employer also agrees to **pay death benefits.**
4. In return, the executive agrees to **comply with certain conditions of employment.**

The essential elements of the plan, then, are a two-way agreement and some practical way of making sure that funds for payments will be available when needed.

What does a typical employer-employee contract cover? The contract is prepared by an attorney, with the employer generally agreeing:

1. To employ the executive in a stated capacity and to pay a current salary as agreed upon.

2. To begin paying on a certain retirement date a specified amount of deferred salary from a stated number of years.
3. To continue the payments to the spouse or other beneficiary for a guaranteed number of years, if the executive dies after retirement but before receiving all of the payments.
4. To pay a death benefit to the spouse if the executive dies before retirement.

On his or her part, the executive usually agrees:

5. To stay with the company for a certain number of years (normally until retirement).
6. To withhold his or her services from any competing company during retirement.

How is the plan funded? It is assumed that all payments under the plan will be made from the company's earnings or surplus. So the company exercises good judgment when it sets up reserves that will tend to offset the costs of the plan. Life insurance is ideally suited for this purpose. Here are the typical life insurance arrangements:

1. The **key executive is insured** under a type of policy and in an amount the company feels is suitable.

2. The **type of policy** depends on the benefits **guaranteed** under the contract of employment. If death benefits are provided, a life paid-up at 65 policy has the advantages of
   a. paying the face amount in case of death,
   b. being paid for at the normal retirement date and
   c. having substantial cash to help in paying retirement income.
3. The **amount of the policy** is more or less **optional.** Complete funding would imply that the policy be in an amount necessary to reimburse the company for anticipated premium payments plus the net, after-tax outlay for benefits payable under the plan. (For example, if a corporation is in a 34 percent tax bracket, and if the contract calls for payments of $10,000 a year from the employee's age 65 to 75, the gross liability for benefits is $100,000—but the net, after-tax liability is only $64,000. If a life paid-up at 65 policy were used, a completely funded plan would require an amount of insurance equal to the $64,000 after-tax cost of benefits plus total premiums to age 65.) **As a practical matter, the company may adjust the amount of insurance in accordance with the amount of premium it is willing and able to pay.**
4. The policy is **purchased by, owned by and payable to the company.** Cash values and eventual

death proceeds become part of the company's general assets.

5. At the employee's retirement, the company **may prefer to leave the policy intact,** pay retirement income out of earnings or surplus and realize the **entire face amount of the** policy when the retired employee eventually dies.

What are the Tax Aspects of the Plan? Although a deferred compensation plan requires no formal qualification with the Internal Revenue Service, the tax advantages under the plan may be disallowed if the plan is not designed to serve a reasonable and proper business purpose—if its main objective is tax avoidance. It is wise to confine deferred compensation plans to **those whose services are so valuable that additional compensation is perfectly justifiable.** When a plan is "clean" in the eyes of the taxing authorities, all persons involved can enjoy tax advantages:

1. Proceeds of the life insurance policy are received by the company **tax free** at the employee's death. This is about the only way a corporation can receive tax-free dollars, and with many corporations in a 34 percent bracket, these dollars are almost doubled in value.

2. The yearly increases in cash value are not subject to income tax.
3. Deferred compensation paid to the retired employee, or payments to the spouse, are **deductible expenses.** Premiums are **not deductible by the employer.**
4. The key executive incurs no additional income tax prior to retirement.
5. After retirement, the key person's deferred compensation is taxable income, but then he or she will have a **double exemption and probably a much lower tax bracket.**
6. The first $5,000 of any death benefits are excluded from the beneficiary's gross income, as long as vested rights to the benefit were not possessed by the employee immediately before death.

Key Sales Points

For the employer, this plan will:

- **attract the services of a much-needed executive** or provide an incentive for a valuable associate to remain with the company.
- **enable you to offer a deferred salary increase** PLUS a substantial **death benefit,** at far less cost than a current salary increase with a greater net income to the executive.

- **provide key-person insurance to help offset the loss of the executive's services,** since insurance proceeds probably will exceed any death benefit payable to the surviving spouse.
- **deliver many thousands of tax-free dollars** to the company at the death of the key executive.
- **create an emergency fund** which can be drawn upon in time of business need or can be used to enhance credit and facilitate outside borrowing. And increases in the fund are nontaxable .
- **greatly improve morale** and loyalty among those staff members who are the mainsprings of the business.

For the key executive, this plan will:

- **give you a substantial retirement income** that could not otherwise be provided under a regular pension plan.
- **make such a retirement plan available at no outlay on your part.** Furthermore if you tried to set up an equivalent income plan yourself, present high taxes on your earned and investment income would make the outlay almost prohibitive.
- **provide very generous benefits to your family** in case of your early death. And these benefits might be very hard to duplicate out of your salary, after taxes.
- **enable you to realize a much greater financial return** for your years of service to the company.

Instead of your taking a raise, most of which might be eaten up by increased taxes, the additional income is deferred until a time when your tax bracket will be lower and your personal exemption doubled.

The Rabbi Trust

An increasingly popular form of deferred compensation is the so-called "rabbi trust," so named because its first application was in the case of a rabbi whose congregation wished to provide a retirement vehicle for him. This type of trust provides some protection for a key employee that is lacking in many deferred compensation arrangements. This is an irrevocable trust that may be funded or unfunded. However, if the employee is to avoid current income tax on any contributions to the trust, the instrument must be declared to be subject to the claims of creditors of the employer in case of a default. The aptly named *secular trust* is a similar arrangement, except that the trust proceeds are secured from inception for the employee and current income taxes must be paid by the intended recipient.

SPLIT-DOLLAR PLANS

Any split-dollar plan embodies the principle of sharing (splitting) the premium outlay. The contributing persons may be employer and employee, father and daughter, father and son-in-law, grandfather and grandson or any other combination of two individuals whose purposes would be served by the plan. In any event, the split-dollar plan has tremendous appeal, since it **permits the insured to carry permanent life insurance at less than term cost**— while there is **no cost or risk to the other person who contributes to the premium payments.**

Two General Types of Plans

There are many premium-splitting arrangements that can be made, but the two most popular plans are based **on the "cash value increase"** principle and the **"level premium"** principle.

The cash value increase split-dollar plan: This type of plan is generally, but not necessarily, confined to employer-employee relationships. In describing the plan, we shall refer to the "employer" and "employee" as the two persons to the agreement. However, there is nothing about the plan that would prevent its being used in a family situation.

Under this plan, **the employee is the insured; the employer is the other person contributing to the premium payments.** The employer pays that part of the premium equal to the annual increase in cash value. The employee contributes the balance of the premium. The employer's payment grows larger year by year until the increase in cash value equals or exceeds the premium. Thereafter, the insured employee makes no further payments toward the premium.

Should the employee die, his or her family receives the face amount **less the cash value.** Although the death benefit decreases each year, the decrease is gradual. Even after 20 years, the insured's family will receive, in most cases, more than 50 percent of the policy's face amount. Thus, the split-dollar agreement gives the insured **much more life insurance protection** throughout the years than if his or her premium contributions were used to buy term insurance.

The employer usually owns the policy and is joint beneficiary. **At the employee's death, the employer receives an amount equal to the cash value,** or whatever amount is left of the cash value if the employer has borrowed any of it. The policy's cash value will **never be less** than the employer's total contributions. It may be **greater** in the later years.

For business situations, the advantages of the split-dollar plan can be summarized as follows:

1. The employer can **single out promising young employees and tie them to the business** by offering them substantial low-cost insurance protection .
2. This can be done at **no cost to the employer,** other than the loss of after-tax interest on the funds invested in premium payments.
3. The company has a **growing emergency fund,** and if the employee leaves, the cash value reimburses the employer for every dollar invested.
4. The proceeds received by the employer and the employee's family are **not taxable.**
5. The employee has practically no income tax liability. Only an amount equal to the one-year term cost of the pure protection, less his or her yearly contribution, is reportable income each year.

The Level Premium Split-Dollar Plan: This type of plan is frequently used in family situations to help a relative in creating a much-needed life insurance estate. For example, a young family man may need considerable extra life insurance to cover his responsibilities, but he finds it impossible to fit the premium into his limited budget. With the cooperation of his father, father-in-law or grandfather, he can acquire the needed family protection for only a modest outlay and at no cost to the person who helps him with the premium payments.

However, the level premium split-dollar plan can be adapted ideally to **business situations.** When used in relation to an employer-employee agreement, it eliminates an objection to the cash value increase plan of splitting premiums. Under the latter plan, the employee is required to make the largest payments in the early years, at the time he can afford them least.

But for the purpose of explaining the level premium type of plan, we shall assume that it is being applied to a family situation wherein a father wishes to help his married son set up a realistic life insurance program.

After determining the amount of insurance needed, the **father and son agree on the amount of premium payment the son can squeeze from his budget,** with the father consenting to assume the balance. The son then applies for insurance on his own life and makes a collateral assignment of the policy to his father. **Each year, the son pays at least the amount of premium agreed upon.** He can always pay more, as improved circumstances permit. **The father pays, each year, the balance of the premium due.**

The son gives the father a note for the father's first-year contribution. Each year, a **new note** is substituted to cover the father's aggregate payments. **If the son dies, the father is repaid, to the extent of the most recent note, out of the insurance proceeds. The son's family receives the balance.**

As in any split-dollar arrangement, the son's death benefit decreases each year. However, the decrease is gradual and in reasonable proportion to his decreasing family responsibilities. (Each year a family man lives means one less year he has to provide future income for wife and children.) And, the decrease may be decelerated if a participating policy is purchased and the **dividends used to provide paid-up additions of life insurance.** Or, the dividends can be applied to reduce the father's payments, as shown in the accompanying illustration.

Depending on the type of policy selected, the cash value may be expected to equal the father's total payments in some future year. At that time, the son can borrow the cash value, repay the father and assume **full ownership and control of the policy.**

There are many reasons why the split-dollar plan is a practical and appealing investment for both father and son. Here are a few:

1. The father gains peace of mind knowing that if his son dies, the responsibility of caring for the son's family will not be on his shoulders but will be shifted to a life insurance company.
2. **There is no cost to the father** unless, out of the goodness of his heart, he wishes to cancel the notes and make a gift of them to his son after a number of years.

3. **The son is able to buy a substantial amount of permanent insurance** while he is still insurable, **at low rates** applicable to his young age.
4. Although the death benefit decreases, the **average level of protection afforded is likely to be far in excess of the amount the son could buy** if he put the same number of dollars into **term** insurance.
5. **If the son's wife becomes a widow, her financial self-respect is preserved.** She and the children will not have to experience the disintegration of family ties and affection .

In summary, the split-dollar plan **neatly solves a dilemma faced by the son and eliminates worry on the part of the father.** The son needs the greatest amount of insurance when he is trying to get a home started and can afford it the least. And, his life insurance needs diminish in later years when he can more readily afford to pay premiums. As for the father, he feels anxiety over the security of his son's family should the son die prematurely. Fortunately, **the split-dollar plan takes care of the problems of both father and son—at reduced cost to the son and no cost to the father!**

SPLIT-DOLLAR PLANS ARE POPULAR

Because they are so simple—easy to set up—without legal problems or tax involvements.

Because both parties to the agreement have everything to gain and nothing to lose.

Because family advantages are so obvious and business reasons are so justifiable.

DEATH BENEFIT ONLY PLAN (DBO)

A death benefit only plan, sometimes known as a widow's benefit, or survivor's income benefit (SIB) or salary continuation plan, is funded by life insurance. The employer agrees that upon the employee's death a specified or determinable benefit will be paid to a survivor.

Payments may be made in a lump sum or installments or some combination thereof. Typically the employer collects the policy proceeds from the insurance company on a tax-free basis, subject to alternative minimum tax conditions. Premiums for the insurance are not deductible but when the benefit is paid, the payment is deductible to the company as an expense.

This unique arrangement is made possible under the Internal Revenue Code, whereby an employer may pay a tax-free sum to the beneficiary of an employee, upon the death of that employee. The tax-free benefit is limited to one $5,000 amount for each employee, regardless of the number of employers. The face amount of the policy may be higher but only the first $5,000 is excludable as a family benefit. The DBO plan can be added to or be part of a deferred compensation arrangement; at retirement the DBO cash values may be used to fund retirement payments.

There are two elements of the plan. **First,** although not required by law, it is advisable to draw up a contract between the employer and the key person which provides that the employer, in consideration of the employee's continued employment, will pay $5,000 to the employee's family if the employee dies while on the payroll. Such a contract is essential from the standpoint of employer employee relations. Each can count on the other to fulfill his or her part of the bargain. **Second,** there must be a **practical method of funding** the employer's obligation under the contract.

The Contract: Only an **attorney** should draft the contract between employer and employee. The agreement should include the employer's consideration (the $5,000 payment to the family), the employee's consideration (continued services), the beneficiary, the manner of payment, right to change beneficiary, cause for termination and any other clauses the attorney deems necessary.

Method of funding the contract: Various methods are possible, **but only one is practical.** To illustrate:

1. **Take the money from surplus.** But employees may die during period of business slumps when the company needs all of its available cash
2. **Borrow the money.** But the loss of key people might injure the business to the extent that credit is withheld. If a loan can be secured, it must be repaid PLUS interest.
3. **Set aside the money.** But that would tie up large sums of money which the business could use to far better advantage.
4. **Accumulate the money gradually.** But that would take a long time, and the need may arise next week, and again next month.
5. LIFE INSURANCE ON THE KEY PERSON. The perfect plan—small yearly deposits, the exact amount of money available at the moment it is needed, with the possibility of a tax-free increase to the firm.

How the Plan Works

The contract is drawn, life insurance in the amount of $5,000 is taken out on the key person (of course, a greater amount may be secured, over the $5,000, for the usual protection against key-person loss), then, assuming the key person dies, the $5,000 proceeds are paid to the employer, who in turn pays $5,000 to the key person's beneficiary.

BUT, here is the unique advantage to the employer: **The life insurance proceeds come tax free, yet when the $5,000 benefit is passed along to the beneficiary, it becomes a tax deductible business expense.** For example, if the employer is a corporation in a 34 percent tax bracket, a tax-deductible item of $5,000 means a tax decrease of $1,700. So in this case, **the act of paying out $5,000 results in a tax-free income to the company of $1,700 less the outlay for premiums.** In most cases it would take ten years or more before total premiums equal the tax savings, without even considering cash value and their effect of reducing the cost.

Not a Substitute for Key-Person Insurance

The $5,000 benefit plan does not offset in any way the company's need for key-person insurance to absorb the shock of such a loss. The $5,000 is for the **benefit of the family;** and an **additional amount** should be placed on his or her life for **the benefit of the firm,** in accordance with the company's estimate of the loss it would suffer at the death of the key person.

Sole proprietors and partnerships, as well as closely held corporations, may take advantage of this plan. Although sole owners and partners are not considered as "employees" under the Internal Revenue Code, they do hire other people and can benefit from the tax-saving and morale building aspects of the plan.

No employer should overlook **a source of income that is tax free** both to the family of a key person and to the business, especially when the plan brings the **extra dividends** of decreasing turnover and increasing the efficiency of top-notch employees.

GROUP LONG-TERM DISABILITY

Less than half of U.S. employers offer long-term disability coverages to employees. This in spite of the fact that employees are more than twice as likely to encounter a long period of disability as they are to die between the ages of 30 and 65. Probably part of the reason for this lack of basic coverage is the mistaken notion that Social Security can take care of this problem. The fact is that workers can expect about 30 percent to 42 percent of salary replacement from this source. More highly compensated employees will receive about 25 percent replacement. Often, an initial application for benefits will be declared ineligible and an appeal can be a lengthy process. There is a six-month waiting period and the average benefit is about $600. The disabled worker must establish proof that the disability will continue for at least one year and that it will prevent work at any job during that period. Social Security disability benefits should be viewed as an adjunct to an employer-provided long-term disability program.

PENSION MAXIMIZATION

Arriving at retirement time, workers receiving payout from a defined benefit plan, or indeed from any annuity type of monthly income, must choose among various options for payment of plan accounts. Choices vary from life only, i.e., a monthly payment that ceases upon death, with no beneficiary provisions, to various plans that yield regular payments continued to a surviving spouse.

Naturally any payments beyond the life of the primary pensioner will reduce the monthly amount paid. For example, the difference between a life-only option and one providing continuing payments to a survivor might cause a monthly payment of $2,000 to be reduced to $1,500 a month. Therefore the cost of providing a benefit for the survivor is $500 a month. The question is, for less than $500 a month could the pensioner purchase life insurance to make up the difference, and opt for the largest monthly benefit payable? If the monthly sum from the pension ceases at death, the life insurance benefit can make up the difference. This arrangement could provide for more flexibility at retirement. If the spouse pre-deceases the pensioner, the life insurance benefit could be paid to children, or the policy could be terminated and cashed in. It is more advantageous for the pensioner to purchase additional insurance a few years previous to retirement, in order to keep premium costs lower. Individual situations need to be examined when proposing this idea, since the mathematics may work out more favorably at some ages and not at others.

12

Practical Charts and Tables

Whether your objective is to sell a life insurance package or a complete program, here is a set of handy reference tables for use in the interview and in working out proposals for:

Retirement plans
Dependency period income
Blackout period income
Mortgage cancellation

Study the tables; see what data is included and the order in which the facts are presented; be able to locate the right figures at the right moment.

Commissioners Standard Ordinary Mortality Table
(Showing Life Expectancy in Years)

Age	Male	Female	Age	Male	Female	Age	Male	Female	Age	Male	Female
0	70.83	75.83	25	47.84	52.34	50	25.36	29.53	75	8.31	10.32
1	70.13	75.04	26	46.93	51.40	51	24.52	28.67	76	7.84	9.71
2	69.20	74.11	27	46.01	50.46	52	23.70	27.82	77	7.40	9.12
3	68.27	73.17	28	45.09	49.52	53	22.89	26.98	78	6.97	8.55
4	67.34	72.23	29	44.16	48.59	54	22.08	26.14	79	6.57	8.01
5	66.40	71.28	30	43.24	47.65	55	21.29	25.31	80	6.18	7.48
6	65.46	70.34	21	42.31	46.71	56	20.51	24.49	81	5.80	6.98
7	64.52	69.39	32	41.38	45.78	57	19.74	23.67	82	5.44	6.49
8	63.57	68.44	33	40.46	44.84	58	18.99	22.86	83	5.09	6.03
9	62.62	67.48	34	39.54	43.91	59	18.24	22.05	84	4.77	5.59
10	61.66	66.53	35	38.61	42.98	60	17.51	21.25	85	4.46	5.18
11	60.71	65.58	36	37.69	42.05	61	16.79	20.44	86	4.18	4.80
12	59.75	64.62	37	36.78	41.12	62	16.08	19.65	87	3.91	4.43
13	58.80	63.67	38	35.87	40.20	63	15.38	18.86	88	3.66	4.09
14	57.86	62.71	39	34.96	39.28	64	14.70	18.08	89	3.41	3.77
15	56.93	61.76	40	34.05	38.36	65	14.04	17.32	90	3.18	3.45
16	56.00	60.82	41	33.16	37.46	66	13.39	16.57	91	2.94	3.15
17	55.09	59.87	42	32.26	36.55	67	12.76	15.83	92	2.70	2.85
18	54.18	58.93	43	31.38	35.66	68	12.14	15.10	93	2.44	2.55
19	53.27	57.98	44	30.50	34.77	69	11.54	14.38	94	2.17	2.24
20	52.37	57.04	45	29.62	33.88	70	10.96	13.67	95	1.87	1.91
21	51.47	56.10	46	28.76	33.00	71	10.39	12.97	96	1.54	1.56
22	50.57	55.16	47	27.90	32.12	72	9.84	12.26	97	1.20	1.21
23	49.66	54.22	48	27.04	31.25	73	9.30	11.60	98	0.84	0.84
24	48.75	53.28	49	26.20	30.39	74	8.79	10.95	99	0.50	0.50

Need for Retirement Income

Chance of Living to Age 65 Life Expectancy During Retirement Years

Age	*Chance of Living to Age 65*	*Age*	*Male Years Expected to Live*	*Female Years Expected to Live*
25	82.10	60	22.62	26.32
30	82.38	65	18.63	21.98
35	82.76	70	14.96	17.87
40	83.30	75	11.72	14.02
45	84.16	80	8.96	10.61
50	85.78	85	6.75	7.77

Based on the 1980 CSO Table and 1983 Individual Annuity Table

The chances of a person living to retirement age are better than 80%. And the older the people get, the better the odds that they will need retirement income. When they reach retirement age, the statistics point to a long road ahead. It will be either rough going or smooth and pleasant, depending on what provision has been made for old age.

The Hard Way To Build Retirement Income

Monthly Interest Income from Various Sums*

Principal	*3%*	*4%*	*5%*	*6%*	*8%*	*10%*
$ 10,000	$ 24.70	$ 32.70	$ 40.70	$ 48.70	$ 64.30	$ 79.70
20,000	49.30	65.50	81.40	97.40	128.60	159.40
25,000	61.60	81.90	101.80	121.80	160.80	199.30
30,000	74.00	98.20	122.10	146.10	192.90	239.10
40,000	98.60	131.00	162.80	194.80	257.20	318.80
50,000	123.30	163.70	203.50	243.50	321.50	398.50
60,000	148.00	196.40	244.20	292.20	385.80	478.20
70,000	172.60	229.20	284.90	340.90	450.10	557.90
75,000	184.90	245.60	305.30	365.30	482.30	597.80
80,000	197.30	261.90	325.60	389.60	514.40	637.60
90,000	221.90	294.70	366.30	438.30	578.70	717.30
100,000	246.60	327.40	407.00	487.00	643.00	797.00

*To the nearest 10-cent level.

Compare these interest figures with annuity rates. A typical annuity based on a $10,000 single premium would yield on a 10-year certain basis option, male age 65, $90.42 per month, and income taxes would be payable on only a portion of that payment.

Investment Yields

This table shows the sum of money that must be invested at the end of each year at various rates of compound interest (after taxes and costs of investment management) to produce $1,000 at the end of a given number of years.

No. Yrs.	*5%*	*8%*	*10%*	*12%*
1	$1,000.00	$1,000.00	$1,000.00	$1,000.00
2	487.80	480.76	476.19	471.69
3	317.20	308.03	302.11	296.34
4	232.01	221.92	215.47	209.23
5	180.97	170.45	163.79	157.40
6	147.01	136.31	129.60	123.22
7	122.81	112.07	105.40	99.11
8	104.72	94.01	87.44	81.30
9	90.69	80.07	73.64	67.67
10	79.50	69.02	62.74	56.98
11	70.38	60.07	53.96	48.41
12	62.82	52.69	46.76	41.43
13	56.45	46.52	40.77	35.67
14	51.02	41.29	35.74	30.87
15	46.34	36.82	31.47	26.82
16	42.26	32.97	27.81	23.39
17	38.69	29.62	24.66	20.45
18	35.54	26.70	21.93	17.93
19	32.74	24.12	19.54	15.76
20	30.24	21.85	17.45	13.87
21	27.99	19.83	15.62	12.24
22	25.97	18.03	14.00	10.81
23	24.13	16.42	12.57	9.55

(Continued)

Investment Yields (Continued)

No. Yrs.	*5%*	*8%*	*10%*	*12%*
24	22.47	14.97	11.29	8.46
25	20.95	13.67	10.16	7.49
26	19.56	12.50	9.15	6.65
27	18.29	11.44	8.25	5.90
28	17.12	10.48	7.45	5.24
29	16.04	9.61	6.72	4.66
30	15.05	8.82	6.07	4.14
31	14.13	8.10	5.49	3.68
32	13.28	7.45	4.97	3.28
33	12.49	6.85	4.49	2.92
34	11.75	6.30	4.07	2.60
35	11.07	5.80	3.68	2.31
36	10.43	5.34	3.34	2.06
37	9.83	4.92	3.02	1.83
38	9.28	4.53	2.74	1.63
39	8.76	4.18	2.49	1.46
40	8.27	3.86	2.25	1.30
41	7.82	3.56	2.04	1.16
42	7.39	3.28	1.85	1.03
43	6.99	3.03	1.68	.92
44	6.61	2.80	1.53	.82
45	6.26	2.58	1.39	.73
46	5.92	2.38	1.26	.65
47	5.61	2.20	1.14	.58
48	5.31	2.04	1.04	.52
49	5.03	1.88	.94	.46
50	4.77	1.74	.85	.41

Think how much a person would have to save and invest for years to create sufficient capital to produce an interest income of the amount needed for living expenses!

Life insurance offers a sure way to create income!

Total Future Earnings
Based on Monthly Income

Age Now	*$1,000*	*$1,500*	*$2,000*	*$2,500*
20	$540,000	$810,000	$1,080,000	$1,350,000
22	516,000	774,000	1,032,000	1,290,000
24	492,000	738,000	984,000	1,230,000
26	468,000	702,000	936,000	1,170,000
28	444,000	666,000	888,000	1,110,000
30	420,000	630,000	840,000	1,050,000
32	396,000	594,000	792,000	990,000
34	372,000	558,000	774,000	930,000
36	348,000	522,000	696,000	870,000
38	324,000	486,000	648,000	810,000
40	300,000	450,000	600,000	750,000
42	276,000	414,000	552,000	690,000
44	252,000	378,000	504,000	630,000
46	228,000	342,000	456,000	570,000
48	204,000	306,000	408,000	510,000
50	180,000	270,000	360,000	450,000
52	156,000	234,000	312,000	390,000
54	132,000	198,000	264,000	330,000
56	108,000	162,000	216,000	270,000
58	84,000	126,000	168,000	210,000
60	60,000	90,000	120,000	150,000

If you had an equivalent value vested in property, you would protect it to the hilt with fire and casualty insurance.

5% Option

Monthly Income for Various Periods of Years from $10,000 Insurance

Yrs.	*Inc.*	*Yrs.*	*Inc.*	*Yrs.*	*Inc.*
1	$852	11	$98	21	$63
2	436	12	92	22	62
3	298	13	86	23	60
4	228	14	82	24	59
5	187	15	78	25	58
6	160	16	75	26	57
7	140	17	72	27	56
8	126	18	69	28	55
9	114	19	67	29	54
10	105	20	65	30	53

(Income figures to nearest dollar level.)

6% Option

Monthly Income for Various Periods of Years from $10,000 Insurance

Yrs.	*Inc.*	*Yrs.*	*Inc.*	*Yrs.*	*Inc.*
1	$856	11	$102	21	$69
2	440	12	96	22	67
3	302	13	91	23	66
4	233	14	87	24	64
5	192	15	83	25	63
6	164	16	80	26	62
7	145	17	77	27	61
8	130	18	75	28	60
9	119	19	72	29	59
10	110	20	70	30	59

(Income figures to nearest dollar level.)

7% Option

Monthly Income for Various Periods of Years from $10,000 Insurance

Yrs.	*Inc.*	*Yrs.*	*Inc.*	*Yrs.*	*Inc.*
1	$859	11	$107	21	$74
2	444	12	101	22	73
3	306	13	97	23	71
4	237	14	96	24	70
5	196	15	88	25	69
6	169	16	85	26	68
7	149	17	82	27	67
8	135	18	80	28	66
9	123	19	78	29	65
10	114	20	76	30	65

(Income figures to nearest dollar level.)

DEPENDENCY AND BLACKOUT PERIOD INCOME

Every parent realizes the necessity of arranging a family or spousal income to provide essential needs for varying periods of time. One of these occasions is providing coverage for a widow and young children during the dependency period before offspring are able to assume adult responsibilities.

Another instance when temporary additional income is needed is the so-called blackout period; the years between death of a breadwinner and the time that the spouse becomes eligible for Social Security payments. The following tables illustrate amounts of insurance that will provide $100 per month for temporary periods of time at varying interest rates.

Example: Assume a blackout period of 21 years from the time the youngest child is 18 until a wife's age 62 (spouse's age at husband's death is then 41), during which no Social Security is paid. For each $100 of monthly income desired (using a 7 percent option) insurance required is $13,500.

Insurance Needed to Provide $100 per Month for Various Periods of Years (5% Option)

Yrs.	*Amt.*	*Yrs.*	*Amt.*	*Yrs.*	*Amt.*
1	$1,150	11	$10,250	21	$15,800
2	2,300	12	10,900	22	16,200
3	3,350	13	11,550	23	16,600
4	4,350	14	12,200	24	17,000
5	5,350	15	12,800	25	17,350
6	6,250	16	13,350	26	17,700
7	7,150	17	13,900	27	18,050
8	7,950	18	14,400	28	18,350
9	8,750	19	14,900	29	18,650
10	9,500	20	15,350	30	18,950

(Income figures to nearest dollar level.)

Insurance Needed to Provide $100 per Month for Various Periods of Years (6% Option)

Yrs.	Amt.	Yrs.	Amt.	Yrs.	Amt.
1	$1,150	11	$ 9,750	21	$14,600
2	2,250	12	10,400	22	14,950
3	3,300	13	10,950	23	15,250
4	4,300	14	11,500	24	15,550
5	5,200	15	12,050	25	15,800
6	6,100	16	12,500	26	16,100
7	6,900	17	12,950	27	16,350
8	7,700	18	13,400	28	16,600
9	8,400	19	13,800	29	16,850
10	9,100	20	14,200	30	17,050

(Income figures to nearest dollar level.)

Insurance Needed to Provide $100 per Month for Various Periods of Years (7% Option)

Yrs.	Amt.	Yrs.	Amt.	Yrs.	Amt.
1	$1,150	11	$ 9,350	21	$13,500
2	2,250	12	9,900	22	13,800
3	3,250	13	10,400	23	14,050
4	4,200	14	10,900	24	14,250
5	5,100	15	11,350	25	14,500
6	5,950	16	11,750	26	14,750
7	6,700	17	12,150	27	14,950
8	7,450	18	12,550	28	15,150
9	8,100	19	12,850	29	15,300
10	8,750	20	13,200	30	15,450

(Income figures to nearest dollar level.)

Unpaid Principal and Total Future Interest Per $10,000 of Mortgage

25-Year Mortgage

	At 7%		At 7½%		At 8%		At 8½%	
IF Mortgage Has Run	*Principal Bal.*	*Future Interest*	*Principal Bal.*	*Future Interest*	*Principal Bal.*	*Future Interest*	*Principal Bal.*	*Future Interest*
0 yrs.	$10,000	$11,200	$10,000	$12,170	$10,000	$13,160	$10,000	$14,170
1 yr.	9,850	10,510	9,860	11,420	9,870	12,360	9,880	13,330
2 yrs.	9,680	9,830	9,710	10,690	9,730	11,570	9,750	12,490
3 yrs.	9,510	9,150	9,540	9,970	9,570	10,810	9,600	11,670
4 yrs.	9,320	8,490	9,360	9,260	9,410	10,040	9,450	10,860
5 yrs.	9,120	7,840	9,170	8,570	9,230	9,300	9,280	10,060
6 yrs.	8,900	7,220	8,970	7,880	9,030	8,570	9,090	9,280
7 yrs.	8,670	6,600	8,750	7,210	8,820	7,850	8,890	8,520
8 yrs.	8,420	6,000	8,510	6,570	8,590	7,160	8,670	7,770
9 yrs.	8,150	5,420	8,250	5,940	8,340	6,480	8,440	7,030
10 yrs.	7,860	4,860	7,970	5,330	8,080	5,810	8,180	6,320

11 yrs.	7,560	4,310	7,670	4,750	7,790	5,180	7,900	5,640
12 yrs.	7,230	3,800	7,350	4,180	7,470	4,570	7,590	4,980
13 yrs.	6,870	3,310	7,000	3,640	7,130	4,030	7,250	4,350
14 yrs.	6,490	2,840	6,630	3,120	6,760	3,430	6,890	3,750
15 yrs.	6,090	2,390	6,230	2,640	6,360	2,900	6,490	3,180
16 yrs.	5,650	1,980	5,790	2,190	5,930	2,410	6,060	2,640
17 yrs.	5,180	1,610	5,320	1,770	5,460	1,950	5,590	2,150
18 yrs.	4,680	1,260	4,820	1,390	4,950	1,530	5,080	1,690
19 yrs.	4,150	940	4,270	1,050	4,400	1,160	4,530	1,270
20 yrs.	3,570	670	3,690	740	3,810	820	3,920	910
21 yrs.	2,950	440	3,060	490	3,160	550	3,270	600
22 yrs.	2,290	250	2,380	280	2,460	320	2,550	350
23 yrs.	1,580	120	1,640	130	1,710	140	1,770	160
24 yrs.	820	30	850	40	890	40	920	50

TRUE VALUE OF A MORTGAGE CANCELLATION PLAN—True value should include **future interest the widow does not have to pay** when insurance wipes out the mortgage balance. **Example:** Suppose a mortgage cancellation plan is set up when a $15,000, 25-year mortgage (61/2 percent) has run two years. If death occurs at once, paying off the mortgage will **save $13,470 future interest payments** ($8,980 × 1.5.). This amount should be added to insurance proceeds to appreciate the true value of the plan.

25-Year Mortgage

IF Mortgage Has Run	At 9% Principal Bal.	At 9% Future Interest	At 10% Principal Bal.	At 10% Future Interest	At 11% Principal Bal.	At 11% Future Interest	At 12% Principal Bal.	At 12% Future Interest
0 yrs.	$10,000	$15,200	$10,000	$17,270	$10,000	$19,430	$10,000	$21,620
1 yr.	9,890	14,300	9,910	16,270	9,920	18,330	9,930	20,430
2 yrs.	9,770	13,410	9,800	15,290	9,830	17,250	9,860	19,230
3 yrs.	9,630	12,550	9,690	14,310	9,730	16,180	9,770	18,060
4 yrs.	9,490	11,680	9,560	13,350	9,620	15,100	9,670	16,870
5 yrs.	9,330	10,830	9,420	12,400	9,500	14,040	9,570	15,730
6 yrs.	9,150	10,000	9,260	11,470	9,360	13,010	9,440	14,590
7 yrs.	8,960	9,180	9,090	10,540	9,200	11,990	9,300	13,470
8 yrs.	8,750	8,390	8,900	9,640	9,030	10,980	9,150	12,350
9 yrs.	8,520	7,610	8,690	8,760	8,840	10,000	8,970	11,270
10 yrs.	8,270	6,850	8,460	7,900	8,620	9,040	8,780	10,190

11 yrs.	8,000	6,110	8,200	7,370	8,380	8,100	8,550	9,160
12 yrs.	7,700	5,400	7,920	6,260	8,120	7,180	8,300	8,140
13 yrs.	7,370	4,730	7,600	5,490	7,820	6,310	8,020	7,160
14 yrs.	7,020	4,070	7,260	4,740	7,490	5,460	7,700	6,210
15 yrs.	6,620	3,460	6,880	4,030	7,120	4,650	7,340	5,310
16 yrs.	6,200	2,870	6,450	3,370	6,700	3,890	6,940	4,440
17 yrs.	5,730	2,330	5,990	2,740	6,240	3,180	6,480	3,640
18 yrs.	5,220	1,840	5,470	2,170	5,720	2,520	5,970	2,880
19 yrs.	4,660	1,390	4,910	1,630	5,150	1,910	5,390	2,200
20 yrs.	4,040	1,000	4,280	1,170	4,510	1,380	4,730	1,590
21 yrs.	3,370	660	3,580	780	3,790	920	4,000	1,060
22 yrs.	2,640	380	2,820	450	2,990	540	3,170	620
23 yrs.	1,840	180	1,970	210	2,100	250	2,240	290
24 yrs.	960	50	1,030	60	1,110	70	1,190	70

ANOTHER EXAMPLE OF THE TRUE VALUE OF MORTGAGE CANCELLATION INSURANCE—A person has just purchased a home and has agreed to an $18,000 mortgage, payable over 20 years at 81/2 percent interest. Should he die tomorrow, an $18,000 mortgage cancellation insurance policy would wipe out the principal plus $19,510 future interest ($10,840 × 1.8), so the **true value** of the plan, today, is $18,000 + $19,510, or $37,510.

20-Year Mortgage

IF Mortgage Has Run	At 7% Principal Bal.	At 7% Future Interest	At 7½% Principal Bal.	At 7½% Future Interest	At 8% Principal Bal.	At 8% Future Interest	At 8½% Principal Bal.	At 8½% Future Interest
0 yrs.	$10,000	$8,610	$10,000	$ 9,330	$10,000	$10,080	$10,000	$10,840
1 yr.	9,760	7,920	9,780	8,590	9,790	9,280	9,800	10,000
2 yrs.	9,510	7,240	9,530	7,870	9,560	8,510	9,580	9,180
3 yrs.	9,230	6,590	9,270	7,160	9,310	7,750	9,350	8,360
4 yrs.	8,940	5,950	8,990	6,480	9,040	7,020	9,090	7,580
5 yrs.	8,630	5,330	8,690	5,810	8,750	6,310	8,810	6,820
6 yrs.	8,290	4,740	8,360	5,170	8,440	5,610	8,510	6,080
7 yrs.	7,930	4,160	8,010	4,560	8,100	4,950	8,180	5,370
8 yrs.	7,540	3,620	7,630	3,970	7,730	4,320	7,820	4,680
9 yrs.	7,120	3,110	7,230	3,400	7,330	3,710	7,430	4,030
10 yrs.	6,680	2,620	6,790	2,880	6,890	3,150	7,000	3,420
11 yrs.	6,200	2,170	6,310	2,390	6,420	2,610	6,540	2,840
12 yrs.	5,690	1,750	5,800	1,930	5,920	2,110	6,030	2,310
13 yrs.	5,140	1,370	5,250	1,520	5,370	1,660	5,480	1,810
14 yrs.	4,550	1,030	4,660	1,140	4,770	1,250	4,880	1,370
15 yrs.	3,920	730	4,020	810	4,130	890	4,230	980

16 yrs.	3,240	480	3,330	540	3,430	590	3,520	650
17 yrs.	2,510	280	2,590	310	2,670	340	2,750	380
18 yrs.	1,730	130	1,790	140	1,850	160	1,910	170
19 yrs.	900	30	930	40	960	40	990	50

15-Year Mortgage

0 yrs.	$10,000	$ 6,180	$10,000	$ 6,690	$10,000	$ 7,300	$10,000	$ 7,730
1 yr.	9,610	5,490	9,620	5,960	9,640	6,420	9,660	6,890
2 yrs.	9,190	4,830	9,220	5,240	9,250	5,660	9,280	6,090
3 yrs.	8,740	4,200	8,780	4,570	8,830	4,930	8,870	5,310
4 yrs.	8,260	3,610	8,320	3,920	8,370	4,250	8,430	3,570
5 yrs.	7,740	3,050	7,810	3,320	7,880	3,590	7,940	3,880
6 yrs.	7,190	2,520	7,260	2,750	7,340	2,980	7,420	3,220
7 yrs.	6,590	2,040	6,680	2,220	6,760	2,410	6,840	2,620
8 yrs.	5,960	1,590	6,040	1,750	6,130	1,900	6,220	2,050
9 yrs.	5,270	1,200	5,360	1,320	5,450	1,430	5,540	1,550
10 yrs.	4,540	850	4,630	930	4,710	1,020	4,800	1,110
11 yrs.	3,750	560	3,830	620	3,910	680	4,000	730
12 yrs.	2,910	330	2,980	360	3,050	390	3,120	430
13 yrs.	2,010	150	2,060	170	2,110	180	2,170	190
14 yrs.	1,040	40	1,070	40	1,100	50	1,130	50

20-Year Mortgage

	At 9%		At 10%		At 11%		At 12%	
IF Mortgage Has Run	*Principal Bal.*	*Future Interest*	*Principal Bal.*	*Future Interest*	*Principal Bal.*	*Future Interest*	*Principal Bal.*	*Future Interest*
0 yrs.	$10,000	$11,600	$10,000	$13,180	$10,000	$14,790	$10,000	$16,450
1 yr.	9,810	10,710	9,830	12,190	9,850	13,700	9,870	15,260
2 yrs.	9,610	9,830	9,650	11,220	9,690	12,620	9,730	14,070
3 yrs.	9,380	8,980	9,450	10,260	9,510	12,190	9,560	12,920
4 yrs.	9,140	8,140	9,230	9,320	9,310	10,520	9,380	11,780
5 yrs.	8,870	7,330	8,980	8,410	9,080	9,510	9,170	10,670
6 yrs.	8,580	6,540	8,710	7,520	8,830	8,520	8,940	9,570
7 yrs.	8,260	5,780	8,410	6,660	8,550	7,560	8,680	8,510
8 yrs.	7,910	5,050	8,070	5,840	8,230	6,650	8,380	7,490
9 yrs.	7,520	4,360	7,710	5,040	7,880	5,760	8,050	6,500
10 yrs.	7,100	3,700	7,300	4,290	7,490	4,910	7,670	5,550
11 yrs.	6,640	3,080	6,850	3,580	7,060	4,100	7,250	4,650
12 yrs.	6,140	2,500	6,360	2,910	6,570	3,350	6,770	3,810
13 yrs.	5,590	1,970	5,810	2,300	6,030	2,650	6,240	3,020
14 yrs.	4,990	1,490	5,210	1,750	5,420	2,020	5,630	2,300
15 yrs.	4,330	1,070	4,540	1,260	4,750	1,450	4,950	1,660

16 yrs.	3,620	700	3,800	840	3,990	970	4,180	1,110
17 yrs.	2,830	410	2,990	490	3,150	570	3,320	650
18 yrs.	1,970	190	2,090	230	2,210	270	2,340	300
19 yrs.	1,030	50	1,100	60	1,170	70	1,240	80

15-Year Mortgage

0 yrs.	$10,000	$ 8,270	$10,000	$ 9,350	$10,000	$10,470	$10,000	$11,620
1 yr.	9,670	7,380	9,700	8,360	9,720	9,380	9,750	10,430
2 yrs.	9,310	6,520	9,360	7,410	9,410	8,330	9,460	9,280
3 yrs.	8,910	5,710	8,990	6,490	9,070	7,300	9,140	8,150
4 yrs.	8,480	4,920	8,580	5,610	8,680	6,330	8,770	7,080
5 yrs.	8,010	4,170	8,130	4,770	8,250	5,390	8,370	6,040
6 yrs.	7,490	3,470	7,630	3,980	7,770	4,510	7,900	5,070
7 yrs.	6,920	2,820	7,080	3,240	7,240	3,680	7,380	4,150
8 yrs.	6,300	2,230	6,470	2,560	6,640	2,910	6,800	3,890
9 yrs.	5,630	1,680	5,800	1,940	5,970	2,220	6,140	2,510
10 yrs.	4,890	1,200	5,060	1,390	5,230	1,590	5,400	1,810
11 yrs.	4,080	790	4,240	920	4,400	1,060	4,560	1,200
12 yrs.	3,190	460	3,330	540	3,470	620	3,510	710
13 yrs.	2,200	240	2,330	250	2,440	290	2,550	330
14 yrs.	1,160	60	1,220	70	1,290	70	1,350	90

30-Year Mortgage

	At 7%		At 7½%		At 8%		At 8½%	
IF Mortgage Has Run	*Principal Bal.*	*Future Interest*	*Principal Bal.*	*Future Interest*	*Principal Bal.*	*Future Interest*	*Principal Bal.*	*Future Interest*
0 yrs.	$10,000	$13,950	$10,000	$15,170	$10,000	$16,420	$10,000	$17,690
1 yr.	9,900	13,260	9,910	14,430	9,920	15,620	9,920	16,850
2 yrs.	9,790	12,570	9,810	13,690	9,830	14,830	9,840	16,010
3 yrs.	9,670	11,890	9,700	12,960	9,730	14,050	9,750	15,170
4 yrs.	9,550	11,210	9,590	12,230	9,620	13,270	9,660	14,340
5 yrs.	9,410	10,550	9,460	11,520	9,510	12,500	9,550	13,530
6 yrs.	9,270	9,890	9,330	10,810	9,380	11,750	9,430	12,720
7 yrs.	9,110	9,260	9,180	10,120	9,250	11,000	9,310	11,920
8 yrs.	8,950	8,620	9,030	9,430	9,100	10,270	9,170	11,140
9 yrs.	8,770	8,000	8,860	8,760	8,940	9,550	9,020	10,360
10 yrs.	8,580	7,390	8,680	8,100	8,770	8,840	8,860	9,600
11 yrs.	8,380	6,790	8,480	7,460	8,590	8,140	8,680	8,860

12 yrs.	8,160	6,210	8,270	6,830	8,390	7,460	8,490	8,120
13 yrs.	7,920	5,650	8,050	6,220	8,170	6,800	8,280	7,410
14 yrs.	7,670	5,110	7,810	5,620	7,930	6,160	8,060	6,710
15 yrs.	7,400	4,580	7,540	5,050	7,680	5,530	7,810	6,040
16 yrs.	7,110	4,070	7,260	4,490	7,400	4,930	7,540	5,380
17 yrs.	6,800	3,580	6,950	3,960	7,100	4,350	7,250	4,750
18 yrs.	6,470	3,110	6,630	3,440	6,780	3,790	6,930	4,150
19 yrs.	6,110	2,670	6,270	2,960	6,430	3,260	6,580	3,570
20 yrs.	5,730	2,250	5,890	2,500	6,050	2,760	6,200	3,030
21 yrs.	5,320	1,870	5,480	2,070	5,640	2,290	5,790	2,520
22 yrs.	4,880	1,510	5,040	1,670	5,190	1,850	5,340	2,040
23 yrs.	4,410	1,180	4,560	1,310	4,710	1,450	4,860	1,600
24 yrs.	3,900	890	4,040	990	4,180	1,100	4,320	1,220
25 yrs.	3,360	630	3,490	710	3,620	780	3,750	870
26 yrs.	2,780	410	2,890	470	3,010	510	3,120	570
27 yrs.	2,150	250	2,250	270	2,340	300	2,440	330
28 yrs.	1,490	110	1,550	130	1,620	140	1,690	160
29 yrs.	770	30	810	30	840	40	880	40

30-Year Mortgage

	At 9%		At 10%		At 11%		At 12%	
IF Mortgage Has Run	*Principal Bal.*	*Future Interest*	*Principal Bal.*	*Future Interest*	*Principal Bal.*	*Future Interest*	*Principal Bal.*	*Future Interest*
0 yrs.	$10,000	$18,980	$10,000	$21,610	$10,000	$24,310	$10,000	$27,040
1 yr.	9,930	18,080	9,940	20,610	9,950	23,210	9,960	25,820
2 yrs.	9,860	17,190	9,880	19,620	9,900	22,120	9,920	24,650
3 yrs.	9,780	16,300	9,820	18,630	9,850	21,030	9,880	23,460
4 yrs.	9,690	15,430	9,740	17,650	9,790	19,940	9,820	22,280
5 yrs.	9,590	14,560	9,660	16,680	9,720	18,870	9,770	21,100
6 yrs.	9,480	13,700	9,570	15,720	9,640	17,810	9,700	19,940
7 yrs.	9,360	12,860	9,460	14,770	9,550	16,750	9,630	18,770
8 yrs.	9,240	12,010	9,350	13,830	9,450	15,710	9,540	17,630
9 yrs.	9,100	11,190	9,230	12,900	9,350	14,670	9,450	16,480
10 yrs.	8,940	10,380	9,090	11,980	9,230	13,640	9,340	15,360
11 yrs.	8,780	9,570	8,940	11,080	9,090	12,640	9,220	14,240

12 yrs.	8,590	8,800	8,780	10,180	8,940	11,640	9,090	13,140
13 yrs.	8,390	8,030	8,590	9,320	8,770	10,670	8,940	12,050
14 yrs.	8,170	7,290	8,390	8,470	8,590	9,710	8,760	11,000
15 yrs.	7,930	6,560	8,170	7,630	8,380	8,770	8,570	9,950
16 yrs.	7,670	5,850	7,920	6,830	8,150	7,860	8,350	8,940
17 yrs.	7,380	5,180	7,650	6,050	7,890	6,980	8,110	7,940
18 yrs.	7,070	4,520	7,340	5,300	7,600	6,120	7,830	6,990
19 yrs.	6,730	3,900	7,010	4,580	7,270	5,310	7,520	6,060
20 yrs.	6,350	3,310	6,640	3,900	6,910	4,530	7,170	5,180
21 yrs.	5,940	2,750	6,230	3,250	6,510	3,780	6,770	4,340
22 yrs.	5,490	2,240	5,780	2,650	6,060	3,090	6,330	3,550
23 yrs.	5,000	1,760	5,290	2,090	5,560	2,450	5,830	2,810
24 yrs.	4,460	1,340	4,740	1,580	5,000	1,860	5,260	2,150
25 yrs.	3,880	950	4,130	1,140	4,380	1,340	4,620	1,550
26 yrs.	3,230	630	3,460	750	3,680	890	3,910	1,030
27 yrs.	2,530	370	2,720	440	2,910	520	3,100	600
28 yrs.	1,760	170	1,900	210	2,040	250	2,190	280
29 yrs.	920	50	1,000	50	1,080	60	1,160	70

THE BIG RETURN ON PREMIUM DOLLARS IF DEATH COMES EARLY

Consider the situation arising in the event of an insured's early death. The return on premium dollars may be fabulous, greatly offsetting any economic trend.

For example, peruse the percentages of possible returns on premium in cases of early deaths as illustrated in the table below (first column on left indicates policy year):

Year Policy Becomes Claim	If premium per thousand of insurance is as indicated, then when policy becomes claim, inflation of each dollar paid in premiums is:				
	$10	$20	$30	$40	$50
1	10,000%	5,000%	3,333%	2,500%	2,000%
2	5,000	2,500	1,666	1,250	1,000
3	3,333	1,666	1,111	833	666
4	2,500	1,250	833	625	500
5	2,000	1,000	666	500	400
6	1,666	833	555	417	333
7	1,428	715	476	357	286
8	1,250	625	417	312	250
9	1,111	555	370	277	222
10	1,000	500	333	250	200

Compound Interest Table

The sum to which **$1 of principal** will increase at various rates of compound interest in a designated number of years:

Yrs.	*5%*	*5½ %*	*6%*	*6½ %*	*7%*
1	$1.05	$1.06	$1.06	$1.07	$1.07
2	1.10	1.11	1.12	1.13	1.14
3	1.16	1.17	1.19	1.21	1.23
4	1.22	1.24	1.26	1.29	1.31
5	1.28	1.31	1.34	1.37	1.40
6	1.34	1.38	1.42	1.46	1.50
7	1.41	1.45	1.50	1.55	1.61
8	1.48	1.53	1.59	1.66	1.72
9	1.55	1.62	1.69	1.76	1.84
10	1.63	1.71	1.79	1.88	1.97
11	1.71	1.80	1.90	2.00	2.10
12	1.80	1.90	2.01	2.13	2.25
13	1.89	2.01	2.13	2.27	2.41
14	1.98	2.12	2.26	2.41	2.58
15	2.08	2.23	2.40	2.57	2.76
16	2.18	2.36	2.54	2.74	2.95
17	2.29	2.48	2.69	2.92	3.16
18	2.41	2.62	2.85	3.11	3.38
19	2.53	2.77	3.03	3.31	3.62
20	2.65	2.92	3.21	3.52	3.87
21	2.79	3.08	3.40	3.75	4.14
22	2.93	3.25	3.60	4.00	4.43
23	3.07	3.43	3.82	4.26	4.74
24	3.23	3.61	4.05	4.53	5.07
25	3.39	3.81	4.29	4.83	5.43
26	3.56	4.02	4.55	5.14	5.81
27	3.73	4.24	4.82	5.48	6.21
28	3.92	4.48	5.11	5.83	6.65
29	4.12	4.72	5.42	6.21	7.11
30	4.32	4.98	5.74	6.61	7.61

Compound Interest Table

The sum to which **$1 of principal** will increase at various rates of compound interest in a designated number of years:

Yrs.	*7½ %*	*8%*	*8½ %*	*9%*	*9½ %*
1	$1.08	$ 1.08	$ 1.09	$ 1.09	$ 1.10
2	1.16	1.17	1.18	1.19	1.20
3	1.24	1.26	1.28	1.30	1.31
4	1.34	1.36	1.39	1.41	1.44
5	1.44	1.47	1.50	1.54	1.57
6	1.54	1.59	1.63	1.68	1.72
7	1.66	1.71	1.77	1.83	1.89
8	1.78	1.85	1.92	1.99	2.07
9	1.92	2.00	2.08	2.17	2.26
10	2.06	2.16	2.26	2.37	2.48
11	2.22	2.33	2.45	2.58	2.71
12	2.38	2.52	2.66	2.81	2.97
13	2.56	2.72	2.89	3.07	3.25
14	2.75	2.94	3.13	3.34	3.56
15	2.96	3.17	3.40	3.64	3.90
16	3.18	3.43	3.69	3.97	4.27
17	3.42	3.70	4.00	4.33	4.68
18	3.68	4.00	4.34	4.72	5.12
19	3.95	4.32	4.71	5.14	5.61
20	4.25	4.66	5.11	5.60	6.14
21	4.57	5.03	5.55	6.11	6.73
22	4.91	5.44	6.02	6.66	7.36
23	5.28	5.87	6.53	7.26	8.06
24	5.67	6.34	7.08	7.91	8.83
25	6.10	6.85	7.69	8.62	9.67
26	6.56	7.40	8.34	9.40	10.59
27	7.05	7.99	9.05	10.25	11.59
28	7.58	8.63	9.82	11.17	12.69
29	8.14	9.32	10.65	12.17	13.90
30	8.76	10.06	11.56	13.27	15.22

Compound Interest Table

The sum to which **$1 of principal** will increase at various rates of compound interest in a designated number of years:

Yrs.	*10%*	*10½%*	*11%*	*11½%*	*12%*
1	$ 1.10	$ 1.11	$ 1.11	$ 1.12	$ 1.12
2	1.21	1.22	1.23	1.24	1.25
3	1.33	1.35	1.37	1.39	1.40
4	1.46	1.50	1.52	1.55	1.57
5	1.61	1.65	1.69	1.72	1.76
6	1.77	1.82	1.87	1.92	1.97
7	1.95	2.01	2.08	2.14	2.21
8	2.14	2.22	2.30	2.39	2.48
9	2.36	2.46	2.56	2.66	2.77
10	2.59	2.71	2.84	2.97	3.11
11	2.85	3.00	3.15	3.31	3.48
12	3.14	3.31	3.50	3.69	3.90
13	3.45	3.66	3.88	4.12	4.36
14	3.80	4.05	4.31	4.59	4.89
15	4.18	4.47	4.78	5.12	5.47
16	4.60	4.94	5.31	5.71	6.13
17	5.05	5.46	5.90	6.36	6.87
18	5.56	6.03	6.54	7.09	7.69
19	6.12	6.67	7.26	7.91	8.61
20	6.73	7.37	8.06	8.82	9.65
21	7.40	8.14	8.95	9.84	10.80
22	8.14	8.99	9.93	10.97	12.10
23	8.95	9.94	11.03	12.23	13.55
24	9.85	10.98	12.24	13.63	15.18
25	10.83	12.14	13.59	15.20	17.00
26	11.93	13.41	15.08	16.95	19.04
27	13.11	14.82	16.74	18.90	21.32
28	14.42	16.37	18.58	21.07	23.88
29	15.86	18.09	20.62	23.49	26.75
30	17.45	19.99	22.89	26.20	29.96

Compound Interest Table

The sum to which **$1 of principal** will increase at various rates of compound interest in a designated number of years:

Yrs.	*12½%*	*13%*	*13½%*	*14%*	*14½%*
1	$ 1.13	$ 1.13	$ 1.14	$ 1.14	$ 1.15
2	1.27	1.28	1.29	1.30	1.31
3	1.42	1.44	1.46	1.48	1.50
4	1.60	1.63	1.66	1.69	1.72
5	1.80	1.84	1.88	1.93	1.97
6	2.03	2.08	2.14	2.20	2.25
7	2.28	2.35	2.43	2.50	2.58
8	2.57	2.66	2.75	2.85	2.95
9	2.89	3.00	3.13	3.25	3.38
10	3.25	3.39	3.55	3.71	3.87
11	3.65	3.84	4.03	4.23	4.43
12	4.11	4.33	4.57	4.82	5.08
13	4.62	4.90	5.19	5.49	5.81
14	5.20	5.53	5.89	6.26	6.66
15	5.85	6.25	6.68	7.14	7.62
16	6.58	7.07	7.58	8.14	8.73
17	7.41	7.99	8.61	9.28	9.99
18	8.33	9.02	9.77	10.58	11.44
19	9.37	10.20	11.09	12.06	13.10
20	10.55	11.52	12.59	13.74	15.00
21	11.86	13.02	14.29	15.67	17.18
22	13.35	14.71	16.21	17.86	19.67
23	15.01	16.63	18.40	20.36	22.52
24	16.89	18.79	20.89	23.21	25.78
25	19.00	21.23	23.71	26.46	29.52
26	21.38	23.99	26.91	30.17	33.80
27	24.05	27.11	30.54	34.39	38.70
28	27.06	30.63	34.66	39.20	44.32
29	30.44	34.62	39.34	44.69	50.74
30	34.24	39.12	44.66	50.95	58.10

Compound Interest Table

The sum to which **$1 deposited each year** will increase at various rates of compound interest in a designated number of years (deposits are made at the end of each year):

Yrs.	*5%*	*5½%*	*6%*	*6½%*	*7%*
1	$ 1.00	$ 1.00	$ 1.00	$ 1.00	$ 1.00
2	2.05	2.06	2.06	2.07	2.07
3	3.15	3.17	3.18	3.20	3.21
4	4.31	4.34	4.37	4.41	4.44
5	5.53	5.58	5.64	5.69	5.75
6	6.80	6.89	6.98	7.06	7.15
7	8.14	8.27	8.39	8.52	8.65
8	9.55	9.72	9.90	10.08	10.26
9	11.03	11.26	11.49	11.73	11.98
10	12.58	12.88	13.18	13.49	13.82
11	14.21	14.58	14.97	15.37	15.78
12	15.92	16.39	16.87	17.37	17.89
13	17.71	18.29	18.88	19.50	20.14
14	19.60	20.29	21.02	21.77	22.55
15	21.58	22.41	23.28	24.18	25.13
16	23.66	24.64	25.67	26.75	27.89
17	25.84	27.00	28.21	29.49	30.84
18	28.13	29.48	30.91	32.41	34.00
19	30.54	32.10	33.76	35.52	37.38
20	33.07	34.87	36.79	38.83	41.00
21	35.72	37.79	39.99	42.35	44.87
22	38.51	40.86	43.39	46.10	49.01
23	41.43	44.11	47.00	50.10	53.44
24	44.50	47.54	50.82	54.35	58.18
25	47.73	51.15	54.86	58.89	63.25
26	51.11	54.97	59.16	63.72	68.68
27	54.67	58.99	63.71	68.86	74.48
28	58.40	63.23	68.53	74.33	80.70
29	62.32	67.71	73.64	80.16	87.35
30	66.44	72.44	79.06	86.37	94.46

Compound Interest Table

The sum to which **$1 deposited each year** will increase at various rates of compound interest in a designated number of years (deposits are made at the end of each year):

Yrs.	*7½ %*	*8%*	*8½ %*	*9%*	*9½ %*
1	$ 1.00	$ 1.00	$ 1.00	$ 1.00	$ 1.00
2	2.08	2.08	2.09	2.09	2.10
3	3.23	3.25	3.26	3.28	3.29
4	4.47	4.51	4.54	4.57	4.61
5	5.81	5.87	5.93	5.98	6.04
6	7.24	7.34	7.43	7.52	7.62
7	8.79	8.92	9.06	9.20	9.34
8	10.45	10.64	10.83	11.03	11.23
9	12.23	12.49	12.75	13.02	13.30
10	14.15	14.49	14.84	15.19	15.56
11	16.21	16.65	17.10	17.56	18.04
12	18.42	18.98	19.55	20.14	20.75
13	20.81	21.50	22.21	22.95	23.72
14	23.37	24.21	25.10	26.02	26.97
15	26.12	27.15	28.23	29.36	30.54
16	29.08	30.32	31.63	33.00	34.44
17	32.26	33.75	35.32	36.97	38.71
18	35.68	37.45	39.32	41.30	43.39
19	39.35	41.45	43.67	46.02	48.51
20	43.30	45.76	48.38	51.16	54.12
21	47.55	50.42	53.49	56.76	60.26
22	52.12	55.46	59.04	62.87	66.99
23	57.03	60.89	65.05	69.53	74.35
24	62.30	66.76	71.58	76.79	82.42
25	67.98	73.11	78.67	84.70	91.25
26	74.08	79.95	86.35	93.32	100.91
27	80.63	87.35	94.69	102.72	111.50
28	87.68	95.34	103.74	112.97	123.09
29	95.26	103.97	113.56	124.14	135.79
30	103.40	113.28	124.21	136.31	149.69

Compound Interest Table

The sum to which **$1 deposited each year** will increase at various rates of compound interest in a designated number of years (deposits are made at the end of each year):

Yrs.	*10%*	*10½%*	*11%*	*11½%*	*12%*
1	$ 1.00	$ 1.00	$ 1.00	$ 1.00	$ 1.00
2	2.10	2.11	2.11	2.12	2.12
3	3.31	3.33	3.34	3.36	3.37
4	4.64	4.68	4.71	4.74	4.78
5	6.11	6.17	6.23	6.29	6.35
6	7.72	7.81	7.91	8.01	8.12
7	9.49	9.63	9.78	9.93	10.09
8	11.44	11.65	11.86	12.08	12.30
9	13.58	13.87	14.16	14.47	14.78
10	15.94	16.32	16.72	17.13	17.55
11	18.53	19.04	19.56	20.10	20.65
12	21.38	22.04	22.71	23.41	24.13
13	24.52	25.35	26.21	27.10	28.03
14	27.98	29.01	30.09	31.22	32.39
15	31.77	33.06	34.41	35.81	37.28
16	35.95	37.53	39.19	40.93	42.75
17	40.54	42.47	44.50	46.64	48.88
18	45.60	47.93	50.40	53.00	55.75
19	51.16	53.96	56.94	60.09	63.44
20	57.27	60.63	64.20	68.01	72.05
21	64.00	68.00	72.27	76.83	81.70
22	71.40	76.14	81.21	86.66	92.50
23	79.54	85.13	91.15	97.63	104.60
24	88.50	95.07	102.17	109.85	118.16
25	98.35	106.05	114.41	123.49	133.33
26	109.18	118.19	128.00	138.69	150.33
27	121.10	131.60	143.08	155.64	169.37
28	134.21	146.42	159.82	174.54	190.70
29	148.63	162.79	178.40	195.61	214.58
30	164.49	180.88	199.02	219.10	241.33

Compound Interest Table

The sum to which **$1 deposited each year** will increase at various rates of compound interest in a designated number of years (deposits are made at the end of each year):

Yrs.	*12½%*	*13%*	*13½%*	*14%*	*14½%*
1	$ 1.00	$ 1.00	$ 1.00	$ 1.00	$ 1.00
2	2.13	2.13	2.14	2.14	2.15
3	3.39	3.41	3.42	3.44	3.46
4	4.81	4.85	4.89	4.92	4.96
5	6.42	6.48	6.54	6.61	6.68
6	8.22	8.32	8.43	8.54	8.64
7	10.25	10.40	10.57	10.73	10.90
8	12.53	12.76	12.99	13.23	13.48
9	15.09	15.42	15.75	16.09	16.43
10	17.98	18.42	18.87	19.34	19.81
11	21.23	21.81	22.42	23.04	23.69
12	24.88	25.65	26.45	27.27	28.12
13	28.99	29.98	31.02	32.09	33.20
14	33.61	34.88	36.20	37.58	39.01
15	38.81	40.42	42.09	43.84	45.67
16	44.67	46.67	48.77	50.98	53.29
17	51.25	53.74	56.36	59.12	62.02
18	58.66	61.73	64.97	68.39	72.01
19	66.99	70.75	74.74	78.97	83.46
20	76.36	80.95	85.83	91.02	96.56
21	86.91	92.47	98.42	104.77	111.56
22	98.77	105.49	112.70	120.44	128.73
23	112.12	120.20	128.92	138.30	148.40
24	127.13	136.83	147.32	158.66	170.92
25	144.02	155.62	168.21	181.87	196.70
26	163.02	176.85	191.92	208.33	226.22
27	184.40	200.84	218.82	238.50	260.02
28	208.45	227.95	249.37	272.89	298.73
29	235.51	258.58	284.03	312.09	343.04
30	265.95	293.20	323.37	356.79	393.78

General Index

A

B

J

K

L

M

N

O

P

R

S

T

V

W

Y

NOTES

NOTES

NOTES

NOTES

NOTES

NOTES

NOTES

NOTES

NOTES

NOTES

NOTES